PANORAMAS OF
LOST LONDON

WORK, WEALTH, POVERTY & CHANGE

1870-1945

PANORAMAS OF
LOST LONDON

WORK, WEALTH, POVERTY & CHANGE
1870-1945

Philip Davies

Foreword by

Dan Cruickshank

CONTENTS

Left: 10-12 Coventry Street, Leicester Square, 17 March 1914

Previous pages:
Left: View of Chelsea and Old Battersea Bridge, c1870
View taken by James Hedderly from the tower of All Saints, Chelsea, prior
to the construction of the Chelsea Embankment.
Right: 9 Eagle Street, Holborn, 8 April 1904

FOREWORD

Photographs can weave a magic spell that transports us through time; they can capture, tantalise and inflame the imagination. And few photographs are more powerfully evocative than those of lost buildings of great cities. The photographs in this book – of London from 1870 to 1945 and almost invariably showing buildings that are now no more – have astonishing emotional power and appeal. Looking through the pages I feel overwhelmed – thrilled, delighted and, of course, despairing. There is much here to reflect upon, much cause for sorrow, for this book reminds in a most startling manner of the great changes that have overtaken London during the last one hundred and forty years, the way its special character has been eroded and of those ancient ways of life that have been lost forever.

These photographs are, like all memorials to lost lives and lost beauty, heartbreaking documents, poignant and moving; but photographs by their nature offer something more, something hard to define. By capturing and framing with clinical precision a fleeting moment in time they keep that moment alive for eternity. They allow us, as if in a time machine, to travel back, to re-inhabit long-lost streets, to look into the faces of those long dead. It is extraordinary, haunting. Photographs, in their rich and varied detail, offer us an intimate yet almost tangible connection with the past, with the buildings and places they show, with the people who happened to flit through the images, their shades just visible in open doors and windows, or who stood and stared at the photographer at the moment the shutter was released. Look for example at the photographs of the Old Farm House in Marshalsea Road – reduced by 1910 to a lodging house for parish paupers – with a ghostly figure set within its decayed late 17th century front door and with beds packed within one of its fine panelled rooms. All now has long been swept away, all would be forgotten if not for these photographs which record not just the appearance of the building but also, in some uncanny way, its atmosphere, its grand but crumbling soul. What could be more evocative than these images, what more effective as a reminder of transience and of the life and death of cities?

Particularly fascinating in this photographic record are those things once taken for granted but which now no longer exist in any significant way; especially striking for me is the humble timber-built vernacular architecture, little more than village buildings, that once stood in central London. There are many examples commemorated in the pages that follow of this now virtually lost type of building. Utterly mesmerising are the small-scale late 17th or early 18th century clapboard houses that once stood in Bartholomew Close, Cloth Fair, Smithfield and the end of terrace affair – complete with Venetian window – that nestled next to the stately late 17th century houses in Wellclose Square, Stepney.

On the purely topographical level this book is a treasure trove for all who know – or aspire to know – London; it is packed with images of buildings that represent now-missing links in the physical story of the city. For example: 37 Cheapside, which was built in 1667 and photographed in 1908, was the best, if not absolutely the last, survivor of the large-scale terrace houses run-up in the City immediately after the Great Fire of 1666; or the long and low late 17th century terrace in Little Wild Street, Holborn, with its area palisades made of wood not iron. Nothing like these buildings now survives in central London.

And then there are the long-gone masterpieces of London's domestic architecture, created by humble and often anonymous builders but which formed artistic high-points in the fabric of the city. Who could look at the sensational photograph of the splendid early 18th century terraces in Mayflower Street, Rotherhithe and not fall victim to a roller coaster of emotion: soaring with elation at the wonder of the street then plunging into desolation at the prospect of all that has gone? And for me it's almost a physical shock to contemplate the 1945 photograph of those strange and fantastic early 18th century houses in Swedenborg Square, Stepney that, because of bomb damage and wanton neglect, were obliterated early in the post-war era along with neighbouring late 17th century Wellclose Square. The loss of these once affluent merchant enclaves, together with that other merchant bastion of Spital Square (also illustrated in this book), are among the most grievous demolitions of post-war London. The only joy we now have in them is that they are documented by these splendid photographs and so can live in our imaginations.

As well as revealing lost buildings and places of great interest and character *Panoramas of Lost London* also captures the ephemera of city life – the shopfronts, posters, hoardings, street lamps and all those once-ordinary things recorded in these photographs as if by accident. The set of images of Norton Folgate, Spitalfields and Bishopsgate taken between 1909 and 1912, are a wonderful example of the visual variety of even modest city streets, while the wall of posters at Westminster Bridge Road in 1907 takes us straight to the heart of Edwardian London.

Technology also plays a key role in the spell cast by early photographs. Plate cameras on tripods, with superb lenses and large glass negatives, made images that are so precise they can be enlarged to reveal stunning details, and shutter speeds were soon fast enough to capture even moving people with clarity. These early photographs can, when enlarged as in this book, reveal so much detail that you feel surrounded, engulfed, almost as if you were actually there. So, even if the actual buildings cannot be brought back to life, this evocative and haunting book is the next best thing; like its many photographs, it too is pervaded by an intangible magic.

Dan Cruickshank
London, Spring 2011

Opposite: 1-5 Westgate Street, Hackney, 28 October 1904

INTRODUCTION

Lost London 1870-1945 opened windows on a vanished past and revealed a London unknown to many; one which was tantalisingly familiar, yet hauntingly remote. Spanning 75 years from the mid-1870s to 1945, it depicted a world in the throes of transformational change – from the horse-drawn Victorian and Edwardian city through the inter-war years to the devastated streets and buildings of the wartime capital.

Using pictures taken by photographers of the London County Council (LCC) as buildings and areas were on the threshold of redevelopment, they show Georgian and Victorian London as it was vanishing. One of the underlying narratives of the book was the epic struggle of the conservation movement from its early antiquarian beginnings into a mass movement for managing change. London was in the vanguard of the movement to save historic buildings and places from destruction, and photographers were in the forefront of recording what was being lost.

In 1875 the Society for Photographing Relics of Old London was formed to record vanishing mediaeval survivals. This was followed by a group of enlightened individuals who, in 1900, formed the London Survey Committee, which in turn was absorbed later into the LCC. As buildings and streets were awaiting redevelopment, in an astonishingly far-sighted move, LCC photographers were despatched to capture a permanent record of them. Each full plate photograph is an individual work of art in its own right – suffused with rich sepia tones which convey a remarkable level of detail. The spectral figures of people and vehicles are the product of long exposure times, which add even more to the ghostly quality of the images; echoes perhaps of our own mortality.

In the spring of 2010 English Heritage mounted an exhibition of highlights from *Lost London* at Kenwood House. Enlarged to poster size, for the first time the fine quality of the photographs was revealed, attracting record numbers of visitors entranced by what they saw. It proved so popular that subsequent exhibitions were held in St James's for the London Festival of Architecture, and at City Hall for the Mayor's Story of London Festival.

Following overwhelming interest from the media and the public, over 300 of the photographs have been enlarged and over 60 new pictures added, so that people can enjoy the extraordinary treasures contained within them. The resulting changes in cropping and detail have revealed an astonishing depth of detail. Forgotten people frozen in time live again. Haunting faces randomly bestowed with immortality stare at the camera. Hoardings and shopfronts reveal their wares; and architectural details and textures leap into focus, enhancing the sense of "shock and awe" that Marcus Binney identified when reviewing *Lost London* in *The Times*. The result is a revelation.

Panoramas of Lost London follows four recurring constants in London's history which formed the main themes of the Kenwood exhibition – Work, Wealth, Poverty and Change.

London owes its very existence to the twin pillars of trade and commerce. It has thrived by being an open city capable of assimilating waves of newcomers, who in turn have enriched and enhanced the commercial life of the capital. The wealth created by generations of successful people and businesses has given tangible form to many of its most familiar buildings and places, and endowed a huge range of institutions – from the great City guilds and bastions of intellectual endeavour, like the Royal Institution, to charitable almshouses for the poor, and even humble horse troughs for the weary beasts of burden which one serviced the whole city.

London was, and still is, united by its very diversity; a city of extraordinary extremes of wealth and poverty with rich and poor neighbourhoods closely juxtaposed. It has always been restless; a constantly-shifting kaleidoscope of change as neighbourhoods have declined, prospered or been reconstructed with bewildering rapidity.

As the pace of change has accelerated, so too has public concern at the destruction of historic buildings and places. From its early antiquarian beginnings, conservation grew into a popular movement linked to progressive ideas of town planning and philanthropy. Statutory protection was achieved only gradually in the face of fierce opposition from vested interests. It was not until 1947 that a national system for listing buildings was introduced, and 1971 before prior consent was required for their demolition or alteration. Conservation areas were introduced in 1967, but in spite of this many fine buildings were lost as a result of idealistic post-war planning. Paternalistic attitudes allied with architectural hubris led to a chronic failure to appreciate the very qualities that made London unique and the devastation of so many historic places. In 1966 Ian Nairn wrote: "Of all the things done to London this century, the soft-spoken, this-was-good-for you castration of the East End is the saddest".

Today we are able to strike a better balance between change and continuity, but there is no room for complacency. Over 500 historic buildings are still at risk from neglect and decay. Over 80 conservation areas are declining. With the spectre of climate change an ever-increasing reality, the adaptation and reuse of existing buildings is no longer just a cultural imperative, but an environmental one. Conservation and sustainability are simply two sides of the same coin.

Each generation mourns the passing of the places it values – its own particular vision of London. And we are no different. In 1926 another *Lost London* was published grieving for the loss of what that generation cherished. It was prefaced with a plangent lament:
"O! London won't be London long,
For 'twill be all pulled down;
And I shall sing a funeral song
O'er that time-honoured town"
(Attributed to Maginn: *Lost London* 1926).
But in some ways the quote is misleading. In spite of all the changes of the past century, London still remains recognisably London, thanks in no small measure to small groups of determined individuals who have had the courage to fight and secure a future for the past. But the more London changes, in many ways, the more it seems to remain the same. The ghosts of the past recur again and again in the same places to hold subsequent generations in their thrall; what Peter Ackroyd has called "chronological resonances".

In Whitechapel, for instance, in spite of massive changes over the past 100 years, the streets are still stalked by the twin spectres of poverty and vice. Whitechapel as a whole still remains a great reception area for immigrants who now make up 40% of London's population. Today it is home to a thriving Bengali community, but 120 years ago it was a refuge for the Jews of Eastern Europe displaced in the pogroms of Tsarist Russia. Two hundred years before that, the same houses provided salvation for Huguenot refugees fleeing persecution in France. Chronological resonances like these weave a rich and complex tapestry across time itself, infusing places with layer upon layer of meaning. The present is indeed the child of the past.

"These are houses whose souls have passed in to the limbo of time leaving their bodies in the limbo of London"
(John Galsworthy).

Opposite: Trafalgar Square, 14 February 1913
A pea-souper, photographed at 12.05pm.

WORK

London is built on commerce and trade; an economic constant that echoes across generations.

In the first half of the 20th century London was indisputably the world's greatest metropolis; the cosmopolitan capital of the British Empire at the moment of its greatest extent. It financed half the world's trade, but was also the world's largest workshop and its greatest port. It was the focal point of its road and rail network with an intricate web of transport links radiating from the pulsating heart of the capital. But it was also the country's primary cultural centre with a spectacular concentration of museums and galleries containing world-famous collections from all quarters of the globe.

In 1910 London lay unchallenged as the pre-eminent world city; the economic dynamo that powered Britain and its Empire. A hundred years later, in spite of the vicissitudes of the global economy, if London were a country it would rank within the top 15 world economies with a GVA (Gross Value Added) greater than that of Russia or Saudi Arabia. Together with New York and Tokyo, London remains one of three world cities, and arguably it is still the greatest.

In 1901 40% of its workforce was employed in manufacturing and 60% in retail, transport and the construction industry. Over the previous century a sinuous ribbon of wharves, warehouses and workshops lined the Thames and its tributaries; a chaotic agglomeration of timber yards, ships' chandlers, copper and lead works, generating stations, breweries and factories (p90). London was also the country's main manufacturing centre with a worldwide reputation for quality and excellence and an industrial output that exceeded that of Manchester, Birmingham, Liverpool or Glasgow.

The docks were the largest single employer, but by 1900 cut-throat competition had pushed many dock companies to the brink of collapse. Nine years later they were subsumed into the new Port of London Authority which regulated dock labour and regenerated London's maritime trade from its palatial new headquarters in Trinity Square, the construction of which necessitated the clearance of a whole district around Savage Gardens and Trinity Square (pp216-217).

Until the 1960s with the advent of containerisation and their relocation down river, the produce of the world poured through London Docks – tea, cocoa and coffee; sugar, ivory, silk and tobacco; softwoods from the Baltic, hardwoods from Africa, exotic fruits from the colonies, grain and cattle from Canada and refrigerated meat from Argentina and Uruguay. As late as the 1970s the cavernous riverside warehouses of Wapping and Southwark were laced with the pungent aroma of nutmeg, cinnamon, cardamom and camphor from the tropics (pp72-73).

London's great strength lay in the extraordinary diversity of its economic base – paramount not just in manufacturing and trade, but in commerce and international financial services too. In 1911 Charles Booth wrote "London is supreme not only in variety, but in total magnitude". The great shipping, insurance and banking houses of the City managed Britain's vast overseas investments from magnificent temples of commerce which increasingly replaced the older domestic-scaled buildings of the 18th and 19th centuries.

In 1851 the resident population of the City of London had been 129,000, many of whom were shopkeepers, craftsmen, tailors and artisans. A great deal of manufacturing still took place over the shop and in small backyard factories and workshops, but by 1901 its population had shrunk to 27,000. Many small traders and craftsmen migrated to the City fringe, or to new, purpose-built premises in the Lea Valley, Park Royal and the expanding suburbs. By 1905 four-fifths of the entire City had been rebuilt in the past 50 years, doubling the amount of floorspace for banks, insurance companies, shipping agents and brokers, who oiled the wheels of global and imperial commerce. The City's residential population was replaced by armies of office workers, who commuted daily via the great railway termini and on the underground, and later the deep tube.

Across London teeming neighbourhoods of high-density housing supported large numbers of local shops, home-based businesses and sweated trades in small local workshops and backyards (p59). Over 20,000 young women were employed as casual seamstresses in the fashion houses and tailoring shops of Soho and the West End to cater for the sartorial whims of high society. London's myriad urban villages fostered particular clusters of manufacturing activity – furniture-making in Shoreditch, leather in Bermondsey, pianos in Camden Town, jewellery in Hatton Garden, clothing in Soho, East Marylebone and Whitechapel, second-hand cloth and paper around Smithfield, and printing and publishing around St Paul's – as older trades like ship-building and silk-weaving declined. As late as the Second World War, there were around 40,000 factories in inner London employing over 740,000 people. All of this was connected and serviced by a vast transport network of haulage contractors, carmen, and costermongers who provided the lifeblood of the capital and who can be seen in the photographs going about their daily business (p83 and p213).

Opposite: London Fire Brigade Headquarters, Southwark Bridge Road, April 1929

Opposite: Gatehouse to the Church of St Bartholomew the Great, Smithfield, 18 November 1908
The 16th century, timber-framed entrance gate overlaid with later Georgian brickwork and sash windows. Evans and Witt, stationers, boasts a fine array of pens, paper and greetings cards with an enamel thermometer advertising 'Stephen's Inks – for all Temperatures'. A placard for the *Evening News* promotes the timetable for the King of Sweden's visit. After damage in a Zeppelin raid in 1916, the original frontage was restored in the 1920s.

Above: The Old Dick Whittington Inn, Cloth Fair, 16 May 1904
A fascinating vignette of working London frozen in time. The figures wearing aprons are probably porters from nearby Smithfield Market, whilst the two workmen by the entrance doors could be colliers or labourers. Note the enamel signs for 'Batey's Ginger Beer and Lemonade'. Erroneously described as the oldest inn in London, the Old Dick Whittington was demolished in 1916. The brick building beyond still survives.

Above: 20 Cloth Fair and entrance to Red Lion Passage looking west, 26 March 1912
Note the patriotic paper lanterns for sale in the shop window and the sign for the Fat and Bone merchant on the extreme right. The newspaper placard features 'French Motor Bandits. Three Men Killed'. Wooden scaffolding was common at this time.

Opposite: 51-54 Bartholomew Close, Smithfield, 7 October 1909
The premises of S Crouch & Son, Shop and Office Fitters, general builders and signwriters. No. 51 is occupied by J Potter, a dealer in second-hand cloth and paper, a trade once common in the area. The front wall with the cart behind retains its original wooden posts and railings. The original thick-section glazing bars to the windows are typical early 18th century details.

Opposite: 76 Bartholomew Close, 1927
Small workshops and traders were commonplace in central London well into the 20th century. This shop offered umbrellas for hire for 6d per day. Note the old Crown glass in the shop window and the panelled shutters stacked in front of the shop next door. The stucco pier is chalked with an impression of the latest fashionable hairstyles. Rowntree's pastilles, Boar's Head tobacco and Osram lamps are all familiar British brands.

**Right: Swift's Butchers,
Smithfield Market, 1928**
Swift's spectacular Christmas display of decorated carcasses. A gaggle of geese lie prostrate before an illuminated crib made of lard. A box of sheep's brains can be glimpsed on the central pyramid.

Opposite: 39-40 Norton Folgate, Spitalfields, 25 March 1909
Norton Folgate at Bishopsgate Street Without – the boundary between Shoreditch and the City of London. The elaborate stone boundary plaque is dated 1846. The photographic studio on the extreme left offers coloured or enamelled miniatures for 1/-. The hairdressers is the home of the Norton Folgate Toilet Club. The *Evening News* refers to 'Mind Training For The Boat Race'.

Above: Bishopsgate Street Without looking south from boundary with Norton Folgate, October 1909
Even on the edge of the City of London, the original mediaeval house plots persist filled by 18th and 19th century buildings of a domestic scale and character. Such areas of the City fringe serviced the daily needs of the great temples of commerce further south in the heart of the City. The *Daily Express* placard heralds 'The Budget: Dramatic Decision'.

Opposite: Bishopsgate Street (west side) looking north to Norton Folgate, 7 October 1909
An evocative display of commercial advertising, huge elaborate gas lanterns and elegant shopfronts on the City fringe, which eloquently contrast with the crude banality of so many modern high streets. Lupinsky and Brandon offers 'An Indisputable Fact: Overcoat to measure for 27/6d and Suit to Measure for 30/-'.

Above: Norton Folgate Court House, Folgate Street, 6 October 1909
This late 17th century building became the court house for the manor and liberty of Norton Folgate in 1744. An upper room was used for the court house, and a lower room as a watch house until the abolition of the liberty and its incorporation into the Borough of Stepney in 1900. On the extreme left, beside the corner shop and downpipes, is a fragment of mediaeval stonework alleged to be the remains of St Mary Spital Priory. In the distance is an ice delivery from the North Pole Ice Company.

**Left: Ye Hoop & Grapes public house,
47 Aldgate High Street, c1920**
Flanking the entrance to one of London's oldest
public houses are two ancient carved oak posts,
which can be seen clearly behind the police
constable. The window is screened with raised
and fielded panelled shutters. The butcher's tables
straddle the kerb to drain into the gutter.

Opposite: 48-50 Aldgate, 27 September 1908
This ancient group of 16th and 17th century
timber-framed buildings were occupied by
butchers and eel shops which supplied produce to
nearby City restaurants. It was common for meat
to be displayed in the open air.

Opposite: 4-7 Aldgate, 30 August 1909

The Metropole Restaurant occupied part of a fine 17th century timber-framed coaching inn – the Saracen's Head. On its demolition, the elaborately carved pilasters were salvaged by the Guildhall Museum. At first floor level the Ladies Select Dining Room provided secure facilities at no extra charge for the growing number of working women. Harris's Restaurant catered for a different clientele. Beside the bunches of bananas in the windows of Levy's shop is the entrance to Saracen's Head Yard. On the other side the display of postcards is attracting intense interest.

Right: 7 Jewry Street, Aldgate, 20 August 1909

No. 7 Jewry Street was built in 1650, and survived both the Great Fire and the Blitz before succumbing to a fire in 1946. J E Sly & Son, a well-known firm of rope, sack and bag manufacturers, occupied the house from the early 19th century. The figure in the first floor window is probably one of the Sly family. Next door J Jones dairy has a fashionable marbled plinth and pilasters and applied lettering divided by the central glazing bar.

Above: 190 and 192 Bishopsgate, 22 August 1912
A fine pair of early 18th century town houses in mixed use. The floors over the Empire Restaurant advertise Allbrights Artificial Teeth with coloured globe lamps over the windows denoting a dental surgery. Next to Reynolds and Eason, estate agents, is the Elephant Trading Company of Johannesburg. The arrival of the photographer has provoked widespread interest, but the little girl in the foreground wearing a high-crowned paper hat seems oblivious to the cameraman.

Opposite: 280-282 Bishopsgate, August 1912
Elaborate gilt and glass fascias were commonplace at this time. Saqui and Company is embellished with an ornate Art Nouveau shopfront, a curved glass entrance and mahogany display cases. The building above is a timber-framed 17th century house with a canted central bay decorated with signwriting.

Opposite: 37 Cheapside, 27 September 1908

Built in 1667-68, and still with its original casement windows, this was the earliest surviving example of a house erected immediately after the Great Fire. Beneath the second floor window is a carved tablet depicting The Chained Swan, the name of the tavern which once occupied the building. The True Form Boot Co has fine gilt and glass art nouveau fanlights. Each floor of each building is occupied by a different local business demonstrating the inherent versatility of the London town house.

Above: 11 King Street, 23 March 1912

Small City retailers trading from the ground floor of an early Georgian house with a City cab in the foreground. The poster behind the cab for the *Amateur Gardener* offers advice on 'What to do in your garden at Easter'.

Above: 26-27 Fish Street Hill, Billingsgate, c1913
Ramshackle 18th century houses supported by raking shores. Evans's Stores was typical of the small traders surrounding Billingsgate Market offering sundries for fishmongers. The placard for *The Fishing News* heralds 'Billingsgate New Extension Opening Ceremony', while the *Daily Sketch* and *Daily Express* focus on the crisis in the coal industry.

Opposite: 18-19 Fish Street Hill, Billingsgate, c1913
No. 18 is a genteel house of around 1700 with a general store on the ground floor catering for the working needs of the adjacent fish market. The advertisement for removals with 'Work Done With Covered Motors' and the prominent painted telephone number on the printers next door signal the future.

Opposite: 72 Leadenhall Street, 30 August 1909

The north side towards the eastern end. The Metropole building appears to be an altered 17th century house with a central timber bay. The curious slashes in the shop blind are probably to prevent water collecting as run-off from the bay above. The City gentlemen to the right are sporting summer boaters. In the upstairs window two young office girls appear to have spotted the photographer.

Above: Crutched Friars, 20 June 1912

View along Crutched Friars from New London Street looking east towards the end of Fenchurch Street station. To the right is the side of St Olave's, Hart Street, the model for 'St Ghastly, Grim' in Dickens's "The Uncommercial Traveller" with Seething Lane beyond. On the pavement is a cast-iron fire alarm pillar, once a common item of street furniture, now entirely vanished. The bracketed lantern carries the street name at the top. Keene's is advertising 'Shilling Dinners with Steak and Kidney Pudding on Friday'.

SAMUEL BAGSTER & SONS Limited 15

PATERNOSTER ROW

94

THE
BAGSTER
Bible Warehouse

THE
BAGSTER
BIBLE WAREHOUSE

JUST PUBLISHED.
SIMPLIFIED
HELPS TO BIBLE KNOWLEDGE.
ILLUSTRATED BY ORIGINAL SKETCH MAPS CHARTS & DIAGRAMS.
32 pages 2d NET.

**Opposite: 15 Paternoster Row,
St Paul's, 18 August 1908**

The area around Paternoster Row was one of
the great centres of the English book trade
specialising in educational and religious
books. Samuel Bagster's Bible Warehouse was
typical; an elegant 18th century shopfront
with angled mirrors to each bay to reflect
light into the windows above. The postcards
behind the entrance door depict English
cathedrals. 32 pages of 'Simplified Helps to
Bible Knowledge' could be obtained for 2d.

Right: Old Change, St Paul's, 16 May 1912

View south towards the spire of St Augustine's
Church. Until catastrophic damage in the
Blitz, large areas of the City of London
retained their mediaeval scale and myriad
small businesses in domestic buildings. Here
the carriageway is only wide enough for a
single vehicle piled high with crates. The
typewriter supplier to the right boasts that
they 'Don't Need To Exaggerate. The Truth
is Sufficient'. The site is now occupied by the
futuristic New Change shopping complex
designed by Jean Nouvel.

Left: The Old Blue Last public house, Dorset Street, 3 November 1904

A typical City public house catering for a wide range of clientele from City businessmen in bowler hats to working men in cloth caps. Above the simple ground floor frontage, enriched with applied lettering for popular brands of spirits, is an early Georgian façade.

Opposite: Apothecaries' Hall, Blackfriars Lane, 16 November 1911

The main buildings at Apothecaries' Hall from 1661-71 are arranged around a central courtyard, parts of which rest on the ancient stone walls of the old Blackfriars monastery. The Still Room depicted here was where medicines and pharmaceutical products were prepared for public use.

Left: Apothecaries' Hall, Blackfriars Lane, 16 November 1911
The huge central grindstones used in the preparation of medicines.

Opposite: Apothecaries' Hall, Blackfriars Lane, 16 November 1911
The vaults to the little cellar showing apothecaries' jars and bottles in straw-lined panniers for bottling the medicines produced by the Guild.

Left: 71-76 Fleet Street, 28 March 1912
A group of 18th and 19th century
buildings in multiple use as newspaper
offices, workshops, engravers and
hairdressers, prior to clearance for
street improvements. Signwriting
and advertisement boards across the
façades of buildings were commonplace
until the introduction of controls over
advertisements.

Opposite: 39-59 Strand,
November 1924
The Strand in its heyday with domestic-
scaled buildings of various periods
on their original mediaeval plots and
a wealth of fascinating detail. On the
splayed corner, Vaughan's is promoted as
The Gun Market of the World. Firearms
were relatively easy to obtain at this
time, although following the Firearms
Act 1920 certificates were required for
their purchase and ownership.

Above: Strand, 14 April 1902
View from the south side looking west to St Mary-le-Strand with the buildings on the north side awaiting demolition for the Holborn–Strand improvement scheme. To the right the posters promote the latest ladies' fashions alongside Capstan cigarettes 10 for 3ᵈ and the proud boast that 'Bovril repels Influenza'.

Opposite: Strand, 1902
The dignity of labour. Huge teams of navvies were responsible for the building of a new London. The photograph is carefully posed with the professionals – the surveyors and clerks of works – to the fore. All are wearing hats or caps depending on their social status. The topmost advertisement on the hoarding behind offers a special express service to Paris in 7½ hours.

Opposite: 3 Houghton Street, Aldwych, c1906

The late 19th century was the heyday of ornamental signwriting before the advent of neon. H West occupied this fine bowed shopfront with decorative Ionic columns to the entrance and fluted Greek pilasters to the window. To the right is the narrow entrance to Clare Passage. A M Skinner, a Book Edge Gilder on the upper floors has a brass plate by the door.

Above: 8-11 Houghton Street, 5 August 1906

The hat shop at No. 9 advertises 'Gentlemen's Hats Polished for Sixpence'. To the right, the jars over the shop fascia denote a hardware dealer selling oil for domestic use. The carriageway in the foreground is being relaid with a tarred wood block surface by 'The Improved Wood Pavement Company'. Wood blocks generated less noise than granite setts. To the left at No. 8 is another signwriter, a ubiquitous trade, which supported a thrusting advertising industry.

Opposite: 11 Sheffield Street, 3 May 1904
The dilapidated premises of M Jewell, Waste
Paper and Bottle Merchants with an ancient
ogee-shaped lantern over the door. There was a
ready market for any items of value which could
be recycled and sold. The Masonic symbols
in the upper panels of the shop window mark
the proximity to Freemasons' Hall, while the
wholesale bookseller next door serves the nearby
Inns of Court and Royal Courts of Justice.

Right: Bear Yard, 11 June 1906
With coal as the principal source of energy
for both domestic and commercial buildings,
chimney sweeps were in great demand. Unswept
chimneys frequently caught fire and were a
constant safety hazard. Here the Riland family
can be seen outside their house in squalid Bear
Yard. Note the very narrow entrance door to their
house at No. 12 on the left.

Above: Little Queen Street, Holborn, 11 June 1906

Little Queen Street was swept away for the creation of Kingsway. To the extreme left is the side elevation of the famous Holborn Restaurant with High Holborn beyond. The corner shop is dealing in second-hand furniture. Adjacent is an early roller shutter. Increasingly, these replaced detachable panelled timber shutters to protect shopfronts.

Opposite: Featherstone Buildings, Holborn, 17 August 1908

Featherstone Buildings was a fine composition of two early 18th century terraces between High Holborn and Bedford Street. It was badly damaged by bombing and later demolished for post-war offices. Similar houses survive in Great James Street to the north of Theobalds Road. This is a view of the east side looking north. The gabled building in the distance still survives as a public house. Note the setted road surface and the St Giles Board of Works lamp columns. Recently these have been recast at the author's instruction as part of the enhancement of Lincoln's Inn Fields.

**Left: Woburn Buildings,
2-14 Dukes Road, Euston, c1920**
Woburn Buildings remains one of
London's most picturesque places.
Built to serve the grand houses on the
adjacent Bedford Estate, they form
part of Thomas Cubitt's original design
of 1822 with a beautiful sequence of
curved bay windows to the shops. Milk
and fresh farm produce were brought
into the great railway stations daily;
hence the line of milk churns on the
footway, which still retains the original
massive York stone slabs over the
cellars beneath.

**Opposite: Brownlow Mews,
Holborn, c1925**
Working London. Mews were service
roads to houses on the main frontages.
Originally used primarily for stabling,
by the early part of the 20th century
they accommodated a wide range of
industrial uses, workshops and garages
for motor vehicles. Today many have
been converted into residential use.

**Opposite: Bedford Chambers,
Covent Garden, 26 September 1921**
Built between 1629-37 to the design
of Inigo Jones, Covent Garden was the
first square to be laid out in London. By
the late 18th century, the buildings had
been progressively redeveloped. Bedford
Chambers, 1877-79 by Henry Clutton,
echoed Jones's original design. The lamp
standard to the left marked the entrance
to an underground public convenience
for market traders in the basement of
Thomas Archer's once magnificent
Baroque mansion of 1716-17 built for
Admiral Russell. The arched gable of the
Floral Hall can be seen in the distance
with the top of its original dome just
above the roofline.

**Left: Bedford Chambers,
Covent Garden, 26 September 1921**
The view from within the arcade of
Bedford Chambers towards King Street
is little altered today. The Great Western
Railway had a receiving office here. Note
the impressive phalanx of brass plates by
the door to the right.

**Left: Floral Hall,
Covent Garden, c1925**

London's markets were the bustling
trading centres of the city, spawning a
rich and vigorous sub-culture offering
produce from across the world –
here, pears, plums and apples from
Australia. Built between 1858-60 by
E M Barry in pre-fabricated cast-iron,
the Floral Hall broke into the main
Piazza with an arched elevation, which
can be glimpsed on p52. The eastern
part was restored in 1997-99 as part of
the Royal Opera House development.
The arched frontage to the Piazza was
dismantled and later reconstructed as
part of Borough Market.

**Opposite: Earlham Street, Seven
Dials, 17 August 1908**

The north side of Earlham Street
looking east towards Seven Dials.
London was once renowned for the
spontaneity of its street life and the
vibrancy of its street markets, many of
which have now vanished. Exuberant
iron lanterns carried on massive
ornamental brackets were a common
feature of the townscape. The three
buildings to the left survive.

Left: Earlham Street, Seven Dials, c1913
The north side of Earlham Street at the east end. A typical London market scene with a wealth of period detail. In the window of The Rose and Three Tuns is a poster for the Imperial Services Exhibition at Earl's Court, and enticing advertisements for beers, cyder, ales and stouts. A £15 reward is offered for a lost single stone diamond ring. "Diplomacy" is on at Wyndham's Theatre. In the background The Crown public house still stands in the corner, but in common with many London neighbourhoods, the spontaneous street life captured in the foreground has been lost.

Opposite: Denmark Street, St Giles's, 18 August 1908

A view of the south side, which remains recognisable today. A number of the early 18th century houses survive. The buildings to the extreme left at the entrance to Flitcroft Street remain. Beneath the pediment Elms Lester Painting Works is the only remaining theatrical scene painting workshop in the West End. From the 1920s Denmark Street was Tin Pan Alley – the birthplace of popular music publishing.

Right: Denmark Place, St Giles's, c1908

Denmark Place is a narrow passage behind the north side of Denmark Street, which housed a range of small workshops. Behind No. 27 was a blacksmith's forge. The back of the forge chimney is not bonded to the wall to minimise the risk of fire.

**Left: 13 & 14 Archer Street, Soho,
20 May 1908**
The upper floors of many Soho houses
were given over to workshops, often
serving the larger West End stores,
particularly the rag trade. In this case the
two women are engaged in upholstery
and trimming for the furniture trade.

**Opposite: 37-39 Carnaby Street, Soho,
18 October 1944**
A remnant of old Soho. Part of a group
of late 18th century houses, No. 37 was
used by an ironmonger and oilman. Note
the oil jar standing on the shop fascia
between the first floor windows and the
sign denoting keys cut. At the south end a
narrow passage can be seen which led to
Pugh's Place, a dingy backland enclave.

Main picture: Oxford Circus, 19 October 1910

Oxford Circus was, and remains, a vibrant focus of London's West End, and the central node of one of the world's great shopping streets. This view from the north-west corner shows the juxtaposition of horse-drawn and motorised vehicles on setted street surfaces. The taxis boast swanky white-walled pneumatic tyres. A new electric arc lamp can be seen in the centre of the road.

Above: 26-30 Regent Street, 23 November 1911

View of the east side of Regent Street close to the junction with Piccadilly Circus which can be glimpsed to the extreme left. Railway booking offices for parcels and goods regulated the lifeblood of the nation. The poster for the London and South West Railway promotes the health benefits of its destinations - "In the Path of the Sun".

Opposite: 14-16 Regent Street, 4 August 1914

Showrooms for new products, such as motor cars produced by the French firm Panhard and Levassor, sought out prominent locations. The Dunlop Rubber Co next door carries the royal warrant over its segmental pediment. An improved wood pavement is being laid on the carriageway, whilst dray horses pulling a cart of Ind Coope deliveries wait patiently in the side street.

Above: St James's Market, Haymarket, 6 November 1908

St James's Market was built in 1663-66 to serve the newly-planned quarter around St James's Square. Rebuilt by Nash in 1817-18, the modest brick dwellings were levelled in 1916. The passageway in the distance led into the Haymarket. The Toilet Saloon has a fine display of Player's Navy Cut cigarettes in the window. The board outside lists the prices for coal, coke and wood, while the placard for *The Star* declares 'Murder in the Borough'.

Opposite and above: 34 Haymarket, 7 December 1908

Fribourg and Treyer, purveyors of snuff and tobacco, began trading in 1751, but closed in
1977. The delightful bow-fronted shopfront, the oldest in London, with its separate side
entrance to the upper floors and wrought iron grilles, still survives as a gift shop, but it has
lost much of its original character. The delicate Adam period screen which divided the rear
part of the shop from the front remains in situ in the new shop.

Above: View of the shop interior and fittings looking towards the street.

Opposite & right: 3 St James's Street, c1920
Established in 1698, Berry Bros and Rudd is Britain's oldest wine and spirit merchant. By the mid-18th century the firm supplied the coffee houses of St James's, which later became gentlemen's clubs such as White's and Boodles. Famous visitors were weighed on the giant weighing beams, seen in the foreground, and their weights recorded in ledgers including Lord Byron, Beau Brummell and Pitt the Younger. The interior remains substantially unaltered. The firm continues to supply the royal family.

Right: The rear room of Berry Bros within No. 1 Pickering Court.
This shows the shop parlour and secret cupboard.

Right: Westminster Bridge Road, 1907
The flank elevation to Gerridge Street
is covered in a magnificent array of
contemporary posters, which were
characteristic of Edwardian London.

Opposite: Baltic Wharf,
Millbank, 25 March 1909
Shipbreaking continued on the Thames
well into the 20th century. Castle's was
a local landmark until 1941 when the
yard was bombed and its extraordinary
collection of naval artefacts destroyed. The
main entrance, seen here, was guarded
by figureheads from HMS *Edinburgh* and
HMS *Princess Royal*. A cartouche from
HMS *Black Prince* can be seen over the
legend "Britannia Rules the Waves".

Main picture: Pool of London, c1914
In 1914 London was the greatest port in the world. A panoramic view of the Pool of London shows the river crowded with shipping. The tower of the Church of St Magnus the Martyr is in the centre of the picture with the Monument to the right. The vast mass of Cannon Street train shed obscures the view of St Paul's which can be seen in the haze on the horizon.

Right: Shad Thames, c1910
Much of the river was lined by vertiginous warehouses creating dark canyons separated by slit-like alleys leading to ancient stairs, jetties and wharves. At Shad Thames a myriad iron bridges spanned the street to allow goods to be moved across the walkways to warehouses inland.

Left: Bankside, 16 May 1912
View looking west from No. 46 towards the power station, warehouses and wharves which characterised an area once known as London's backyard. The house next to British Lion Wharf, which survives, was allegedly occupied by Sir Christopher Wren so he could watch St Paul's arising directly opposite. The setted road surface is littered with horse dung: a recurrent nuisance and health hazard.

Main picture: Guy's Hospital, St Thomas's Street, December 1934
In 1724 Thomas Guy, the son of a wharfinger endowed the hospital for incurables which bears his name. The fine wrought iron railings and gate piers of 1741 frame the pedimented centrepiece which was transformed by Richard Jupp in 1774. The niches contain statues of Aesculapius and Hygieia with allegorical figures on the pediment. An alcove from London Bridge was relocated to one of the courtyards in 1904.

Right: Southwark Fire Station, Southwark Bridge Road, c1908
Police, fire and ambulance stations overtly expressed the ideals of public service and civic pride. Southwark Fire Station was one of the most impressive. The splendid Gothic range in the distance housed the HQ of the Metropolitan Fire Brigade, but it was damaged in the Blitz and later demolished. However, the adjacent Engine House and tower survive, together with an Arts & Crafts extension of 1911.

Opposite: Southwark Fire Station, Southwark Bridge Road, c1908
The Engine House with the Metropolitan Fire Brigade in all its glory ready for action with a horse-drawn appliance in the centre. The same bays are in use today inscribed above with the initials of the Metropolitan Fire Brigade, the Metropolitan Board of Works and the date 1878.

Opposite: Southwark Fire Station, Southwark, c1910
Scaling ladder drill in the courtyard. In the background are parts of the workhouse building erected in 1777 for St Saviour's parish.

Right: Southwark Fire Station, Southwark, 1908
The centre of operations; the telephone switchboard in the Watch Room.

Left: 146-154 Borough High Street, c1905

For centuries, Borough High Street was the principal approach to the City of London from the south. It was lined with coaching inns and yards which conferred a very distinctive character.

These 17th century timber-framed houses were typical of the area. Chaplin's was a dealer in India rubber, gutta percha and protective clothing. Chaplin's lantern advertises 'Leggings and Driving Aprons' with a sign for 'Bath Chair and Perambulator Tyres' in the window beneath.

Main picture: 142-154 Borough High Street, 20 September 1908

Nos. 142-144, with its distinctive parapet frieze of swags and bucrania, was designed by Sir John Soane. Through the central archway was a long, narrow passage lined with terraces and four semi-detached houses built for Francis Adams by Soane in 1785 – hence the inscribed panel over the entrance reading Adams Place. The name was altered later by some wag to Eve's Place. The Far Famed Sausage Co Restaurant offers 'Rump Steak for 5d and Sausages and Mashed for 2½d'. The shopfronts are all protected with demountable panelled timber shutters which were stored inside during opening hours.

Left: 216-224 Borough High Street, c1905

No. 220 is an ancient timber-framed house given over with its neighbour to the production of domestic hardware and equipment. No. 216 to the extreme right is suffering from structural movement with bowed window heads and cills.

Opposite: 309-317 Borough High Street, c1903

A classic group of 17th century houses with projecting central bays and horizontal sash windows to the gables. The picture eloquently portrays the extraordinary range of details commonly found in the Edwardian high street – elegant signwriting, gilt and glass fascias, applied lettering to shopfronts and spectacular ornamental ironwork. Angled lanterns, which were suspended from fascias and designed to throw light back on to shop window displays, have now vanished from London's streets.

Right: 156-162 Long Lane, Bermondsey, 6 February 1913
A splendid display of contemporary posters and advertisements on a mixed group of buildings at the south-west end of Long Lane. No. 158 and the cottages to the left are boarded up awaiting redevelopment together with a large vacant plot at the rear.

Opposite: Queen Square, Finsbury Avenue, Shoreditch, c1905
Situated on the northern fringe of the City of London, Queen Square was a narrow courtyard of early 18th century houses off Finsbury Avenue, close to Broad Street Station. W H Brooks, a chimney sweep and carpet beater, poses outside the grand pedimented doorcase to the house, which has fallen on hard times.

Left: 11 Pitfield Street, Hoxton, c1905
This ancient late 17th century house was a
hardware shop. The engaged oil jars denote a
dealer in oils. The shop window is stacked with
Sunlight and Lifebuoy soaps.

Opposite: 42 Alma Road,
Bethnal Green, 24 May 1909
The weavers' houses of Bethnal Green were
highly distinctive, often only one room deep, with
irregular fenestration patterns and long horizontal
weavers' lights. Good light was crucial for the
delicate art of silk weaving and colour matching,
but by 1909 silk weaving was in sharp decline.
The front half of the room shows spreading out
machinery and hand looms.

Left: 195 Mile End Road, 12 November 1944
A rare weatherboarded timber house of c1700 which housed Halls, a saddler and harness maker. By 1944 horse transport was in terminal decline, spelling the end for many suppliers. No. 195 was demolished shortly after this photograph was taken.

Opposite: 223 Bow Road, 19 November 1909
M Howes was an old established corn and flour dealer selling animal feed, horse mixture, straw and hay from a double-bay 17th century house. Marooned by the post-war Bow flyover, remarkably the building still exists; one of the oldest in the East End.

Opposite: Harbour Master's House, Broadway Wharf, Limehouse, c1900

Maritime London. The river was the pulsating heart of London's economy teeming with lightermen, mariners, dockers and boatmen. Picturesque groups of historic buildings lined whole stretches with jetties and staircases on to the foreshore evoking scenes from Dickens's *Our Mutual Friend*.

Above: 93-101 Three Colt Street, c1900

Textures of the past. This remarkable street scene epitomises London at the dawn of the 20th century with stone pavements, setted streets and small local shops in old vernacular buildings. Weatherboarded houses were once common in inner London, but today only a few fragments remain. Siebert's, with its queue of children outside a well-stocked shop window, was one of two German bakers in the street.

**Left: Albert Road, North Woolwich,
21 March 1899**
The densely-packed neighbourhoods of
the East End supported large numbers
of local shops catering for a whole range
of daily needs. R Hodge was a general
dealer stocking household provisions
including cheese, bacon, vegetables, tea,
chocolate and black fuel for coal fires.

**Opposite: 52 Dace Road, Old Ford,
8 December 1904**
F Crooks' local corner shop with a
splendid array of enamel advertisements
promoting a whole range of products,
most of which are familiar today.

ROBIN
THE NEW
Starch.

Grate
Polish

Reckitt's
Blue

NESTLÉ'S
THE
RICHEST
IN
CREAM
SWISS
MILK

PROVISIONS & ❖ F. CROOKS. ❖ CONFECTIONERY

SUNLIGHT

ICE CREAM   R.WHITE'S HOT DRINKS   ICE'D DRINKS

·52·

R.WHITE'S CAKES

R.WHITE'S
HOP ALE
A MAGNIFICENT BEVERAGE

Lehmann's
ENAMELINE

R.WHITE'S
Soda Water
ABSOLUTELY PURE

Lehmann's

R.WHITE'S
LEMONADE   ENAMELINE

SUNLIGHT

R.WHITE'S
GINGERETTE
DELICIOUS WINTER DRINK

R.WHITE'S
PEPPERMINT
DELICIOUS WINTER DRINK

R.WHITE'S
STRAWBERRY
DELICIOUS WINTER DRINK

R.WHITE'S
RASPBERRY
DELICIOUS WINTER DRINK

R.WHITE'S
BLACK-CURRANT
DELICIOUS WINTER DRINK

R.WHITE'S
CHERRY BRANDY
DELICIOUS WINTER DRINK

R.WHITE'S
CLOVES
DELICIOUS WINTER DRINK

R.WHITE'S
VANILLA
DELICIOUS WINTER DRINK

R.WHITE'S
CORDIALS
AND
FRUIT SYRUPS
STRONGEST and BEST.

R.WHITE'S
BLACK-CURRANT
DELICIOUS WINTER DRINK

R.WHITE'S
CHERRY BRANDY
DELICIOUS WINTER DRINK

R.WHITE'S
CLOVES
DELICIOUS WINTER DRINK

R.WHITE'S
VANILLA
DELICIOUS WINTER DRINK

CHOCOLATE FRY'S CHOCOLATE FRY'S CHOCOLATE FRY

FRY'S CHOCOLATE FRY'S CHOCOLATE

BRITISH OAK TOBACCO THE BEST

FRY

R.WHITE'S
KAOLA
R.WHITE'S CELEBRATED GINGER BEER
KAOLA

R.WHITE'S
SARSAPARILLA

R.WHITE'S
GINGER BEER

R.WHITE'S
GINGER BEER

R.WHITE'S
GINGER BEER

Above: 75-77 Broadway, London Fields, Hackney, 16 October 1906
The dogs seem more interested in Rosenberg's the family butcher rather than the dog food shop next door, which has a finely-detailed canted bay shopfront coruscated with colourful enamel advertisements. The adjacent firm cleaned and supplied ostrich feathers.

Opposite: 85 Broadway, London Fields, Hackney, 16 October 1906
P J Ryan, tobacconists, with a fascinating amount of contemporary detail. The advertising lantern is angled to throw light on to the shop window which advertises Victory V gums and Fry's chocolate. The *Daily Mirror* announces a major mine disaster in Durham with 30 killed and 150 entombed. The placards carry the latest racing results. *Football Chat* shows that allegations of match-fixing in football are not new.

Right: 98-102 High Street, Fulham, 6 May 1904
A view once redolent of many parts of the inner suburbs: a mixed group of 18th century domestic buildings housing a range of local traders – hair cutting rooms, cobblers, a steam cycle works and sweet shop. "The Fatal Wedding" is showing at the Fulham Theatre.

The entire group was demolished for an extension of the LCC's tramway track from Hammersmith to Putney Bridge in 1909.

Left: 210 New King's Road, Fulham, 5 December 1947
Richard Dwight was granted a patent for the manufacture of pottery
and ceramics in 1672, and for over 250 years Fulham Pottery was
an industrial site at the west end of New Kings Road. The site
was redeveloped in 1979-80, but a 19th century bottle kiln with
its characteristic domed profile was retained. It can still be seen
alongside the new office block.

WEALTH

The wealth created from generations of successful trade and enterprise was invested in buildings which exuded the power and status of their owners. Increasingly, the older merchants' houses of 18th century London, like those in Spitalfields (pp103-105), and the once fashionable houses of the aristocracy in the West End gave way to a new wave of opulent buildings which reflected the rising wealth of the emerging industrial and middle classes.

Philanthropy is a rich, continuous seam permeating London's history. There is a long and noble tradition of wealthy benefactors providing endowments for the poor, the sick and the needy. One of its most tangible manifestations is the foundation of almshouses for the poor, where a lucky few enjoyed decent living conditions in small, sheltered communities. Morden College (p102) was a typical early example, whilst Thomas Coram's establishment of the Foundling Hospital in Bloomsbury (p118) in 1742 created a London institution which saved generations of abandoned children from abuse, starvation and premature death on the streets. The ancient City Livery Companies were particularly active endowing almshouses and schools using their great repositories of wealth for philanthropic ends. Many of the great livery halls in the City – like Drapers Hall (p109) were sumptuously enriched or rebuilt to proclaim the greater glory of their guild.

In the West End, the Freemasons went from strength to strength expanding on their site in Great Queen Street with a whole series of opulent buildings – all of which were swept away in 1927-32, including fine rooms by Sir John Soane and Philip Hardwick, for a colossal new headquarters with even more spectacular interiors by Ashley & Newman.

The surge of new development swept through the West End. The Ritz Hotel in Piccadilly, one of London's first steel-framed buildings, was completed in 1906 to the design of Mewès and Davis, whilst in St James's new discreetly grand gentlemen's clubs replaced the mansions of the aristocracy. The Royal Automobile Club displaced both Cumberland House and Buckingham House in 1911. The Savage Club (pp119-121), renowned for its bohemian antics, moved frequently, whilst older political institutions, like the Conservative Club (pp122-123) were solid bastions of the Establishment.

High society lived in a tightly-defined area of Mayfair, St James's and Belgravia, where life for the social elite of around 7,000 people revolved around the Season opening on the Friday nearest 1 May with the Royal Academy Summer Exhibition and ending in late July after Goodwood. In between were the Derby, Ascot, the Chelsea Flower Show, Wimbledon and Henley, culminating in Queen Charlotte's Ball where debutantes were presented at Court.

Some of the most lavish parties took place in the great aristocratic town houses of Mayfair – like Devonshire House, Dorchester House and Norfolk House (p129), where the sons and daughters of the old landed families could be introduced socially to the new wealth of the industrial and commercial classes.

For the masses, the West End was London's playground – a glittering, vibrant world of the demi-monde, which offered illimitable opportunities for pleasure for all classes. The primary focus of this was around Piccadilly Circus (p132), the heart of the Empire and the hub of London's louche nightlife. The Criterion restaurant (pp133-134) was one of London's largest, its dining room famed throughout the world.

Increasingly the expanding middle classes developed their own style – often wildly idiosyncratic, like William Burges's mediaeval Gothic fantasy, Tower House, in Kensington (pp136-142), built for his own use between 1876-78.

Alongside the more overt expressions of new-found wealth, power remained deeply engrained in many of the older centres. Admiralty House and the Admiralty (pp144-148) with its extraordinary Board Room, remains celebrated as the scene of many of the most momentous events in British naval history. The Royal Institution for the Advancement of Science (pp130-131) founded in 1799 remains in the forefront of national intellectual life, whilst St James's Palace (pp149-151) is still the official residence of the monarch and the court at which Ambassadors pay homage.

As the centrifugal forces driving London's expansion gathered momentum, the once-isolated mansions and villas of the wealthy were subsumed into the great maw; sometimes, like Belsize Lodge (p153) as islands marooned in a sea of new development, but, with rising land values, others like the haunting Gothic Hall in Highgate Road (p152), succumbed to the relentless march of new development.

Opposite: Conservative Club, 74 St James's Street
Drawing room, first floor front.

Above: Morden College, St German's Place, Blackheath, 24 September 1942
Philanthropy is a continuous thread in London's history. It was not uncommon for prosperous
merchants and business men to use their surplus wealth to help those less fortunate. Morden
College was founded in 1695 by Sir John Morden, a Turkey merchant, as almshouses for "decayed
Turkey merchants". Almost certainly designed by Sir Christopher Wren, it forms a handsome
quadrangle. The principal west front, shown here, has the figures of the founder and his wife in a
double niche in the pediment above which rises an open cupola and clock.

Opposite: Spital Square looking towards No. 22 with St Mary's Passage beyond, 3 May 1909
In the early 18th century many prosperous merchants occupied houses close to the City of
London. Nos. 5-9 Spital Square (left) were built as a terrace c1704. Nos. 5 and 6 were remodelled
during the Regency with faux stone-coursed stucco, wrought iron balustrades and an elaborate
iron lamp overthrow to No. 5. Beyond is the German Synagogue (1858) in a heavy classical
style. The cleanliness of the street, the absence of clutter and the innate sense of visual order are
particularly notable.

Opposite: 56 Artillery Lane, Spitalfields, 12 November 1908

The finest surviving mid-Georgian shopfront in London in use as a grocers and general store. The entire frontage is divided into four bays of different widths by Doric three-quarter columns with iron grilles beneath the flat-fronted shop windows which have curved corner bays. Above is a later elegant Regency balcony.

Right: 56 Artillery Lane, Spitalfields, 12 November 1908

The first floor rooms still retain much of their mid-18th century decoration, but sadly this superb carved chimney piece has gone. In this view of the back room the magnificent Chinese rococo chimneypiece can be seen to full advantage with a space left for a picture or mirror. The foliated sides are dripping with carved icicles, but the open pagoda which once crowned the centrepiece has been removed. Note the elaborate gasolier suspended from the ceiling.

Left: St James's Vicarage, Butcher Row, Stepney, 22 March 1945
View of the front elevation showing the effects of enemy action. Built in 1795-96 as the Master's House of the Royal Foundation of St Katharine, possibly by Thomas Leverton, it retains a remarkable series of large mural paintings in the ground floor rooms. Here the original Ionic porch (subsequently restored) has been destroyed by bombing. In the front garden is an Anderson shelter.

Opposite: St James's Vicarage, Butcher Row, Stepney, 22 March 1945
View of the west wall of the Drawing Room showing one of the surviving murals, a classical seascape based on Claude's *Landing of Aeneas* of 1772.

Above: Ludgate Hill, c1905

The pulsating heart of the City of London, the engine of London's wealth, this view looks south towards Ludgate Circus showing the railway bridge and signal gantries of the London, Chatham and Dover railway erected in 1865 in the face of public protest – "a miracle of clumsy and stubborn ugliness". To the right marked by a lavish array of barometer clocks is J W Benson, Steam Factory for Watches and Clocks. The elaborate coats of arms boast patronage by the ruling houses of Greece, Prussia and Russia.

Opposite: Drapers' Hall, Throgmorton Street, c1900

As ancient bastions of wealth and philanthropic benevolence, the City livery companies occupy a unique role in London life. Past members of the Drapers' Company include Sir Francis Drake, Lord Nelson and King George VI. Drapers' Hall boasts one of the most grandiloquent interiors with a wonderful Great Hall altered by Herbert Williams in the 1860s, and enriched by Sir Thomas Graham Jackson in 1898-99.

Opposite & right: National Provincial Bank, Bishopsgate, c1900

The former National Provincial Bank, designed by John Gibson in 1864-65, epitomised the swaggering commercial confidence of the mid-Victorian city. Crowned by allegorical statuary, the superb single-storey frontage is divided into equal bays by refined fluted Corinthian columns with carved panels of relief between. The frontage and main banking hall were retained as part of the wider redevelopment of the site for Tower 42 (the former National Westminster Tower) designed by Richard Seifert in 1970.

Right: The sumptuous interior with red marble columns and friezes of relief sculpture beneath three huge glass domes which flood the banking hall with light. The former banking hall is now a hospitality and conference venue.

Left: 76 High Holborn, c1912
Henry Treadwell and Leonard Martin were responsible
for a wonderfully inventive series of London buildings
which were a cocktail of Tudor, Baroque and Art Nouveau
styles. James Buchanan's, completed in 1909, was typical of
their effervescent mixture of styles. Sadly the building was
destroyed in the Second World War, although its gabled
return in Fetter Lane survives, and can be seen on p233.

Opposite: Freemasons' Hall,
Great Queen Street, Holborn, 15 March 1911
Founded in 1717, the Grand Lodge of England acquired a
house in Great Queen Street in 1774 triggering a complex
series of developments of ever-increasing grandeur. Two
years later Thomas Sandby designed the first purpose-built
masonic hall in England in the form of a Roman Doric temple
enriched with masonic symbols. The Anti-Slavery society was
founded here in 1807, and in 1863 the Football Association
met for the first time in the tavern at the front. Severely
damaged by fire in 1883, Sandby's hall survived until 1933
when it was demolished for a new suite for the Connaught
Rooms designed by Ashley and Newman, the architects of the
colossal new Freemasons' Hall next door.

Opposite: 2-24 Bedford Row, Holborn, 17 August 1908
Much of Georgian and early Victorian London owed its remarkable unity to the standardised approach to elevations drawn up by estate surveyors. The design of the houses and the wider layout of an area were infused with a classical proportional system based on the Imperial system of measures. This can be seen clearly here on the east side of Bedford Row. Note the telegraph wires on the roofs and the valances with retractable external Venetian blinds.

Left: 1 Bedford Square, Bloomsbury, 1 July 1913.
Ground floor rear room. The plain exterior of the London terrace house often concealed ornate, enriched interiors.

Opposite & left: 13 Lincoln's Inn Fields, 1 February 1911

View looking north of the old library and dining room of the Sir John Soane museum designed by Soane in 1812. The central panel of the ceiling representing Aurora was painted by Henry Howard. On his death in 1837 Soane bequeathed his house and collection to the nation as a museum for "the study of Architecture and the Allied Arts". The room remains virtually identical today.

Left: View of the Monument Court of the museum at basement level crammed with architectural fragments and sculptures, much of which was collected in Rome in the 1790s for Henry Holland. The bust on the pedestal is that of Soane.

Opposite: The Foundling Hospital, Guilford Street, Holborn, c1912
The Court Room, with its splendid rococo ceiling by William Wilton, was a repository for some of the finest mid-18th century art in London. The relief panel over the fireplace by Rysbrack depicts charity children gainfully employed in husbandry and navigation. On demolition in 1937, many of the original contents and fittings were salvaged and relocated in a new neo-Georgian building for the Thomas Coram Foundation including the Court Room, chimneypieces and a massive oak staircase from the former Boys' Wing.

Above: Savage Club, King Street, Covent Garden, c1900
The Savage Club was formed in 1857 as a leading gentlemen's club. Members, drawn from the arts, music, drama, literature, science and the law, are known to each other as "Brother Savage". The entrance hall at one of its former homes at King Street reflects the bohemian nature of the club with a characteristically bizarre collection of African masks, spears and trophies.

Right & opposite:
1 Carlton House Terrace, c1910
Designed by John Nash and built between 1827-33 as the termination of his great triumphal route from the Mall to Regent's Park, many of the interiors of the houses were designed by others. No. 1, later the home of Lord Curzon, was by J P Gandy Deering with a splendid staircase screen of paired Ionic columns. Glimpsed to the right behind the column are the trophies of the Savage Club, which occupied the first floor at this time.

Opposite: The first floor dining room laid out ready for the arrival of unruly Savages. The building is now occupied by the Institute of Materials, Metals and Mining.

Right & opposite:
74 St James's Street, 22 April 1945
Designed by George Basevi and Sydney Smirke in 1844 as the Conservative Club, No. 74 is one of the most handsome frontages in an area renowned for its understated, urbane architecture, but here it is looking tired and shabby at the end of the Second World War. The Club closed in 1959. Following restoration, it is now occupied by HSBC.

Opposite: Clubland epitomised. View of the Library with square columns and pedestals of multi-coloured scagliola and gilt mouldings. The leather chairs, mahogany furniture, leather-topped tables and well-stocked library all convey the quiet repose of an exclusive gentlemen's club.

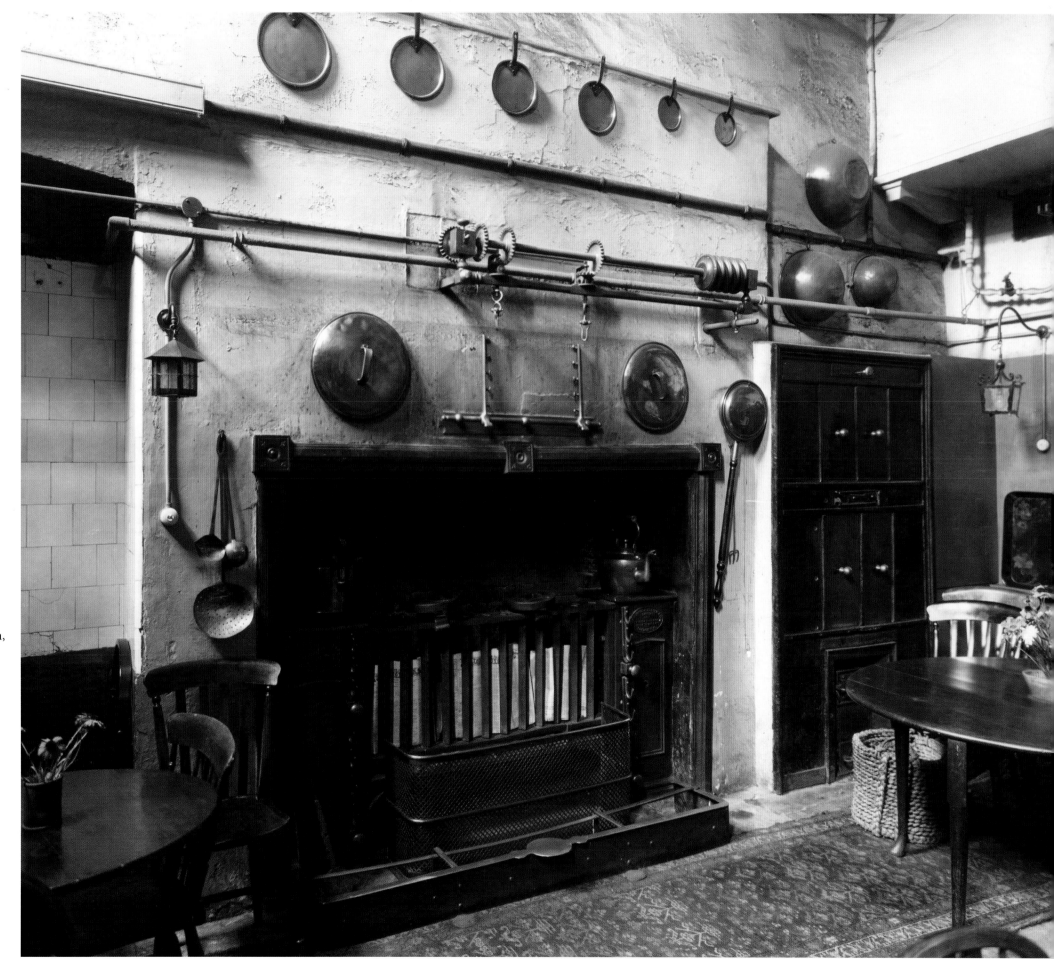

Opposite: 27 Berkeley Square, 1906
Berkeley Square was one of London's most fashionable addresses. The houses on the north side were rebuilt by the Grosvenor Estate in 1820-21 to face the square. With its Chinese cabinet, floral wallpaper and fabrics, the drawing room, shown here, eloquently conveys the fin-de-siècle furnishings and decoration typical of the period.

Right: 45 Berkeley Square, c1910
45 Berkeley Square was the home of Clive of India and boasts rich tropical wood interiors which formed part of his Indian trophies. It was here, after vocal parliamentary criticism, that he committed suicide on 22 November 1774, stabbing himself with his own pen-knife. At the rear of the house is a double-height kitchen, which still survives, shown here with all its accoutrements including a rotating spit and side ovens.

Opposite & right: 22 Arlington Street, c1910

One of London's finest interiors, 22 Arlington Street was built in two phases between 1740-50 by William Kent for his patron, Henry Pelham, who became Prime Minister in 1743. The *tour de force* is this magnificent Great Room with a fantastic coffered ceiling of red and blue panels enriched with grisaille mythological figures. In this view it is cluttered with pot plants, tables and Edwardian furnishings. It has now been incorporated into the adjacent Ritz Hotel.

Right: The front range had a number of forebuildings including this ballroom built in the 1880s for Lord Wimborne. As part of the restoration of 1977-81 the forebuildings were demolished to reinstate Kent's original concept. The bamboo and cane chairs and Chinese jardinière are typical of the period.

Left: 22 Arlington Street, 4 November 1948
The ground floor French room was decorated in the late 19th century in French rococo style with a marble chimneypiece, overmantel and scenes of classical mythology.

Opposite: Norfolk House, 31 St James's Square, c1910
Norfolk House was one of London's great aristocratic town houses with an understated, grand nine bay frontage designed by Matthew Brettingham between 1748-52. This view shows the drawing room with its coffered ceilings and lavish gilded plasterwork designed for entertainment and to impress the visitor with the wealth and power of England's premier dukedom.

Opposite: Royal Institution, Albemarle Street, 8 April 1943

The wealth from London's rapidly growing global commerce funded some of its greatest institutions. The Royal Institution was founded in 1799 by Benjamin Thompson, Thomas Banks and others for the advancement of science. In 1837-38 the windows were regularised, and a grand screen of fluted Corinthian columns with capitals based on the Temple of Mars Ultor was superimposed over a group of earlier 18th century houses by Lewis Vulliamy. In this wartime view, the sign outside the front entrance denotes a bomb shelter.

Right: Royal Institution, 21 Albemarle Street, 29 March 1949

The elegant split staircase of c1775 is probably by John Carr of York with the double lyre pattern, wrought-iron balustrade typical of his work. The marble statue of Michael Faraday, begun by J H Foley and finished by Thomas Brock, presides over the entrance hall. Behind is a bronze cartouche of James Dewar, the chemist and physicist, by Bertram Mackennal. To the left is a large, early 19th century cylindrical electro-static generator.

Opposite: Piccadilly Circus, c1895

The heart of the Empire and the vibrant hub of London's louche nightlife. Albert Gilbert's Shaftesbury Memorial – the Angel of Christian Charity – actually depicts Anteros, the brother of Eros, the god of requited love, who symbolises the selfless philanthropic love of the Earl of Shaftesbury for the poor. The awkward angled geometry of the Circus has always generated challenging traffic problems.

Above: Criterion Restaurant and Theatre, Piccadilly Circus, 26 October 1902

The Criterion was one of London's largest dining rooms with a French Empire style frontage of 1871-74 by Thomas Verity. The arched central entrance led to the famous Long Bar, the setting for the meeting between Sherlock Holmes and Dr Watson in Conan Doyle's famous stories. The superb Byzantine interior of gilded mosaic and American marble was revealed under sheets of plasterboard after decades of neglect during its restoration in 1984. Spiers and Pond were railway caterers, and the Criterion marked their first foray into the West End.

Opposite: Criterion Restaurant, Piccadilly Circus, 1913
The first floor Great Hall of the Criterion at 2.50pm with paired Corinthian pilasters, painted friezes and curved coffered ceilings lit by a central dome. The tables are set for a formal dinner. A small dais has a piano for entertainment.

Above: Slaters, Kensington High Street, 1909
The jams and pickles counter at Slaters was typical of many shop interiors of the period catering for the well-to-do, with elaborate Art Nouveau glazing, mirrored counters and elegant displays of produce.

Opposite & above: Tower House, 29 Melbury Road, Kensington, c1895
Built for his own use by William Burges between 1876-78, Tower House boasts one of the most spectacular interiors in London with superb structural decoration and painted stencilled details in the distinctive High Victorian style, which Burges perfected at Cardiff Castle and Castell Coch. The house remains in private ownership. In this view of the garden front, with Melbury Road beyond, there is little to suggest the mediaeval fantasy that lies within.

Above: Each room had a particular theme. The Library, depicted here, was dedicated to the liberal arts with a full-blown Burgesian Gothic chimneypiece of The Tower of Babel with Nimrod and Queen Grammar sending out elements of speech. Adjacent is a superb cupboard painted with mediaeval scenes beneath an elaborate frieze and ceiling.

Left & opposite: Tower House, 29 Melbury Road, c1895
View of the Dining Room with a painted tiled frieze above marble-lined walls and a typical Burgesian cabinet in the centre.

Opposite: View of the first floor Drawing Room dedicated to Love with wistfully romantic painted friezes and exotic Indian furniture.

Opposite & above: Tower House, 29 Melbury Road, c1895
Burges's own bedroom; a riotous fantasy of inventive Gothic iconography. It was decorated in deep red with convex ceiling mirrors to reflect candlelight. The mermaid chimneypiece is embellished in silver and gold with an unusual sinuous frieze of sea creatures. In the corner is a romantic mediaeval painted cabinet in the characteristic Burges style with his monogrammed initials at the base.

Above: The architect's own bedhead designed by him with a tantalisingly erotic central cartouche in the Pre-Raphaelite style.

**Left: Tower House,
29 Melbury Road, c1895**
View of the entrance front
from Melbury Road with its
distinctive French Gothic tower
and conical roof.

**Main picture: Westminster
Embankment, c1895**
Imperial London with the newly
completed National Liberal Club
to the right and Whitehall Court
beyond. A cabmen's shelter with
a line of hansoms can be seen
in the foreground. The great
departments of state were being
transformed with palatial new
offices which expressed the
political and commercial might
of the British Empire.

929 NATIONAL LIBERAL CLUB.

Opposite: Admiralty House and Old Admiralty, Whitehall, May 1935
The grimy frontage of Admiralty House festooned with decorations for the Jubilee of King George V.
To the front is Robert Adam's first London commission – the colonnaded Admiralty Screen of 1760-
61, terminated by two simple end pavilions with triple niches.

Above: Old Admiralty House, Whitehall, May 1935
The main entrance hall behind Thomas Ripley's portico of 1723-26 is plain and understated with
Doric pilasters and swags above. In the niche is a statue of Nelson by E H Baily (1844), the near life-
sized original model for Nelson's Column. Suspended from the ceiling with the royal crown is a late
18th century lamp which belonged to the old Navy Board.

Opposite: Admiralty House, Whitehall, May 1935
Entrance hall and split staircase to Admiralty House designed by S P Cockerell with a shallow segmented plaster vault and Roman Doric columns framing the staircase. The panel to the staircase is inscribed with the names of the First Lords of the Admiralty.

Right: Old Admiralty, Whitehall, May 1935
The famous Old Admiralty Board Room from which many of Britain's greatest naval victories were directed. The spectacular carved pearwood garlands, trophies and musical instruments over the fireplace are attributed to Grinling Gibbons; the coffered ceiling above of 1786-87 is by S P Cockerell. The focal point of the room is a wind compass (1707-1714) controlled by a weathervane on the roof, and painted with a map of the British seas, coastal waters and allegorical figures.

Above: Admiralty House, May 1935
The groin vaulted kitchen of Admiralty House complete with its range, dresser and kitchen utensils. Naval banquets were prepared here for the First Lord, who occupied the main house above.

Main picture: St James's Palace, 25 July 1907
St James's Palace remains the official residence of the sovereign. Ambassadors are accredited to the Court of St James. Substantial areas of Henry VIII's palace remain including the Gatehouse and Chapel Royal. The Throne Room is the spatial culmination of the State Rooms which were reworked extensively by Nash in the 1820s with enriched coved plaster ceilings. The chimneypiece to the right dates from 1736-37 and was relocated from a library built for Queen Caroline on the site of Lancaster House. The adjacent carved wood drop with garlands of fruit and flowers is by Grinling Gibbons. Beyond the gilded throne canopy lie the doors to the Council Chamber.

Opposite & right: St James's Palace, 25 July 1907
View of the Armoury with an impressive symmetrical display of arms and armour. The fireplace with its quatrefoil frieze is of Tudor origin, but the unusual Arts and Crafts decoration is by William Morris & Co., which executed Philip Webb's designs in 1866-67. The dado, cornice and doors are covered with stencilled interlaced foliage, and the ceiling with stylised sunflowers. Over the door to the right is a display of Prince of Wales feathers.

Right: Detail of one of the St George and the Dragon chandeliers in the Armoury.

Above: Gothic Hall, Highgate Road, 28 June 1909

Outer London provided a bucolic retreat for the wealthy. As London expanded outwards, villas and country retreats were engulfed by the suburbs. A haunting view of The Gothic, or Gothic Hall, once the home of Sir James Williams, and at the time of the photograph the residence of the vicar of St Martin's, Gospel Oak, whose wife ran a ladies' school from their home. The site is now part of the grounds of William Ellis School.

Opposite: Hunters Lodge, 5 Belsize Lane, Belsize Park, 7 September 1943

The designs for this castellated Gothick cottage ornée were exhibited at the Royal Academy in 1810. Designed by Joseph Parkinson for William Tate, a merchant, the Lodge lost most of its grounds with the development of the immediate area in the 1870s. Reduced in size, it is now known as Belsize Cottage and remains in private occupation.

POVERTY

"East London lay hidden from view behind a curtain on which were painted terrible pictures: starving children, suffering women, overworked men; horrors of drunkenness and vice; monsters and demons of inhumanity; giants of disease and despair"

The Life and Labour of the People in London
Charles Booth, 1902

When Charles Booth completed his monumental 17 volume work *The Life and Labour of the People in London*, it was the most comprehensive survey of the social condition of the capital ever carried out. Commissioned to disprove socialist claims that a quarter of Londoners lived in poverty, what it revealed was infinitely worse.

In the golden age of Edwardian England, one third of all Londoners – about 1.8 million – lived below the poverty line. For a further 1 million, life was precariously balanced with just a week's wages between respectability and pauperism. Illness, bereavement or accident could condemn a family to instant destitution. The highest concentration of poverty – 68% – could be found south of the river between Blackfriars and London Bridge followed by Greenwich with 65%.

The worst social conditions – both moral as well as physical – were linked directly to the actual plan and grain of a district. Blind streets, yards and alleys approached via a single entrance tended to harbour the worst extremes of deprivation and crime. Some of these can be seen here (pp187-190) – Dickensian warrens of sunless courts and alleys; houses cheek by jowl with toxic industries; melancholy streets caked in a penitential garb of soot, where the arrival of the photographer was a major event prompting whole families to stand outside their squalid houses in poignant group portraits. Poverty is etched indelibly in to the faces of the people. The very houses carry the stamp of poverty; the brickwork around the doors rubbed smooth from countless arms and shoulders as people took whatever light and air they could. Theirs was a bleak, harsh world of unremitting grind. In 1905 the average age of death in the West End was 55. In the East End it was 30.

"No more dreary spectacle can be found on this earth than the whole of the awful East … the colour of life is grey and drab. Everything is helpless, hopeless, unrelieved and dirty", wrote Jack London in his haunting portrait of the East End - People of the Abyss. Over 1 million people from all corners of the earth were crammed into a vast labyrinth of insanitary streets, courts and alleys, where life was dominated by the daily search for work, food and shelter. It was a place of poverty, hardship, crime and degradation, but one leavened by an indomitable sense of humour and a deep-seated sense of community, a place where people pooled resources to share the basic necessities of life – such as a pair of boots or a simple bonnet.

Across London 300,000 people lived in one-room tenements. Over 900,000 were housed in illegal lodgings or doss houses. Weekly renting was the norm. 90% of the poor had no home they could call their own beyond the end of the week. Often rooms were occupied on a relay system with two or three tenants each occupying the same vermin-ridden bed with the space beneath let on a similar basis. Living conditions for the poor were a shocking reproach to Edwardian England. By 1905 Dr Barnardo had saved over 60,000 destitute children from appalling squalor, vice and degradation, but thousands of the most vulnerable still slept on the streets.

Spitalfields, Stepney and Whitechapel were a huge ethnic melting pot where waves of immigrants settled in a desperate bid to build better lives. For many, London was a hard, unyielding place, but for those who made it, it offered independence, opportunity and freedom; not least freedom for political exiles and radicals to ferment international revolution. Ironically, Mazzini, Garibaldi, Marx and Engels, Litvinov, Kropotkin and Lenin and Stalin, all found sanctuary in the capital of the greatest empire the world has ever known.

But poverty was not just confined to Bankside, Borough and the East End. For centuries the north side of the Strand was characterised by a maze of mediaeval passages and courts. The first wave of bubonic plague began here in 1665. Clare Market and the area around Drury Lane was a notorious slum with a formidable reputation for crime. Living conditions in parts of Westminster were as bad as parts of the East End. Within 500 yards of the Palace of Westminster lay scenes of unimaginable squalor where streets of once-refined 17th and 18th century houses had descended in to use as cheap lodging houses (p170). The ubiquitous pawnbroker provided a vital lifeline to many, offering short-term loans against items of value (p180 and p252).

"London is a shameful tale of two cities. It is the richest capital of Europe, but half our children live below the poverty line. These families are cut off from the life most Londoners take for granted. They are the dispossessed". But this was not written by Charles Booth, Jack London or Charles Dickens. It was the conclusion of an in-depth study in 2010 by the Evening Standard. Today a communal paupers' grave costs £60 for a baby and £270 for an adult. Today 44% of inner London children – 650,000 – live below the poverty line.

Opposite: Grubb Street, Millbank, 21 May 1906

Above: Shepherd's Place archway and Tenter Street, Spitalfields, 10 May 1909

Shepherd's Place archway (1810) provided the sole access to the mean, cramped houses of Tenter Street beyond. Spitalfields was, and remains, an ethnic melting pot for newly-arrived immigrants. Many of those seen here were refugees from the pogroms of Russia and Eastern Europe. Chronic poverty was endemic. Note the young girl in rags in the foreground.

Opposite: St Mary's Passage and Lamb Street from Spital Square, October 1909

No.1 St Mary's Passage was a large, double-fronted merchant's house built in 1733 by Samuel Worrall, a local carpenter. By the mid-19th century it had become a police station, although by the time of these photographs it had descended into multiple occupation as a workshop and lodging house.

Above: Boundary Street, Old Nichol, Shoreditch, 1899
A typical view of the squalid housing found on the notorious Old Nichol Rookery immortalised in Arthur Morrison's novel *A Child of the Jago*. From here criminal gangs preyed on the unfortunate prostitutes who haunted Spitalfields Market to the south. From 1890 the entire area was cleared in stages by the LCC for the new Boundary Estate, the rubble being used to create the raised central gardens at Arnold Circus.

Opposite: Abingdon Buildings, Boundary Street, Shoreditch, c1905
Model housing built by the LCC as part of its slum clearance of the Old Nichol. These elegant new Arts & Crafts style blocks offered amenities undreamt of by the poor souls inured to the slums they replaced, many of whom were displaced further east.

Opposite & above: 22-26 Wellclose Square, Stepney, 30 July 1943
Begun by Nicholas Barbon in the 1680s, Wellclose Square was a bold attempt to create a fashionable enclave east of the Tower. Until the mid-18th century, many of the houses were constructed in a timber vernacular style. By 1943 the west side was largely derelict. Various attempts to save it failed and it was demolished after a public enquiry in 1961. To the right is a wartime street shelter.

Above: The flank and rear elevations showing blast damage.

Left: Helmet Court, Strand, 11 June 1906
For centuries, the north side of the Strand was characterised by a whole series of narrow, mediaeval passages and courts, a handful of which can still be found towards the west end. Helmet Court stood just to the north and west of Somerset House. The narrow whitewashed entrance to the Strand can be seen in the distance. Poverty is etched into the faces of the children in the foreground – a poignant scene all too common in the courts and alleys of inner and central London.

Opposite: Drury Lane, 11 June 1906
The north side of Drury Lane looking east towards Wych Street in the distance. The narrow entrance to Harford Place can be seen marked by posters. The ragged children in the foreground show the single entrance to Nags Head Court, which is still in occupation even though the street frontage has been demolished.

Above: 1 Clare Market, Aldwych, 21 May 1906

Clare Market was notorious as "one of those filthy, dilapidated rookeries that clung desperately to a sordid existence amid a changing environment". It was well-known for its prize-fighters and as a hotbed of criminal activity, but "a sort of romantic aura attached to the locality … from the old world air permeating the surrounding houses" (*Old Time Aldwych*, 1903).

The junction of Houghton Street and Clare Market. To the right, a watchful constable is keeping an eye on proceedings.

Opposite: Harford Place, 11 June 1906

Approached via a narrow entrance opposite the rear of the Theatre Royal, Drury Lane, Harford Place led to a service yard. The once elegant early 18th century terrace on the south side with ground-floor Venetian windows is boarded up awaiting demolition.

**Left: Sardinia Place,
Lincolns Inn Fields, 11 June 1906**
Warehouses and industrial buildings
could be found cheek by jowl with
rundown houses in multiple occupation.
It was commonplace for children to wear
hats – cloth caps for boys, and boaters in
the summer for girls.

**Main picture: Great Wild Street,
Holborn, 11 June 1906**
View looking south to Sardinia Street
with a sequence of dilapidated shopfronts.
The Perseverance Fish Bar and several
others are vacant pending demolition,
but the milk is still being delivered.
The children are clustered outside the
sweetshop. The young boy in the centre
appears to be holding two animal bones.

Opposite: Little Wild Street, Holborn, 11 June 1906
View looking north-east towards Sardinia Place. To the right is a remarkable group of
original houses erected about 1690 with box gutters and timber balustrading to the front
areas. Beyond is the Baptist Chapel and Mission Hall.

Above: Lamb's Conduit Passage, Holborn, 23 March 1912
View looking east along Lamb's Conduit Passage from the north-east corner of Red Lion
Square. The corner building to the left of the picture was a mixed infants' school which
accounts for the large numbers of children gathered outside in the rain. Conway Hall,
built for the South Place Ethical Society, now occupies the north side of the passage.

Opposite: Parker Street, Westminster, c1905

View east along Parker Street towards Princes Street. The heart of old Westminster was notorious for its chronic poverty. Within 300 yards of the gates of the Palace of Westminster, Parker Street was typical of the squalor which was a standing rebuke to the national conscience until well into the 20th century. By 1905 these early 18th century terraces had fallen into use as cheap lodging houses.

Right: Wood Street, Westminster, 19 October 1909

The south-west corner of Wood Street at the junction with Tufton Street looking west. All are well-shod and most have hats or caps which suggests a group of respectable working families rather than the indigent for which the area was notorious. The entire neighbourhood was redeveloped between 1900-39.

Opposite & above: Blewcoat School, 23 Caxton Street, Westminster, c1910
Built in 1709 by a local brewer, William Green, the Blewcoat School was endowed for the education of fifty poor boys from the local parish "likely to thrive by scholarship". In the niche over the entrance is a figure of a Blewcoat Boy. Behind are bleak tenements from which many pupils were drawn. The school closed in 1939. It is now the gift shop and information centre of the National Trust.

Above: The interior of the school; a single pine-panelled room over a semi-basement united by a modillion cornice and entablature with two niches flanking the entrance. To the left, children's chairs and desks are stacked beneath delightful friezes depicting nursery rhymes.

Above: 38-40 Tufton Street, Westminster, 21 May 1906

A once-handsome pair of early 18th century houses in use as lodging houses. The photographer appears to have attracted keen interest with faces at virtually every window and children gathered together at the entrance to the alleyway. Colonel Blood, who attempted to steal the Crown Jewels in 1671, is reputed to have retired to the previous house on the site with a royal pardon and a pension, fuelling suspicions that he had been acting on behalf of the King. The house was distinguished by a carved brick shield and coat of arms, but was demolished for the buildings seen here.

Opposite: York Buildings, Millbank, 21 May 1906

Living conditions in parts of Westminster were as bad as parts of the East End. By 1906 this squalid series of hovels was no longer fit for human habitation and had been given over to the storage of costermongers' barrows. Life in foetid courts like these must have been unbearable with little light or air. Whitewashing was common to increase reflected light.

Main picture: Pennington Street, Wapping, December 1906
This long range of late 17th century dwellings stood directly opposite the towering walls and warehouses of London Docks, which they pre-dated. Hence the raised level of road surface which provided access to the Docks. The East End labyrinth engulfed many older buildings, such as these, and offered rooms and lodgings for the working poor, who are gathered here outside their houses.

Above: 70-80 Red Lion Street, Wapping, 10 October 1904
Red Lion Street was a long, narrow street which lay at the heart of old Wapping, pre-dating the construction of London Dock in 1805. The southern half, once known as Anchor and Hope Alley, was lined with mean lodging houses and small shops catering for the teeming population of the area. The poster on the grocer's shop reads 'Solving the Fiscal Question? Our Food will cost you Less', the sign of a community struggling to subsist.

Opposite: 89-95 Ropemakers Fields, Limehouse, c1900

The eastern end of Ropemakers Fields at its junction with Nightingale Lane. The left-hand pair of early 18th century houses have once-elegant Georgian shopfronts, No. 89 with a sinuous double bow. George Morrow and Son was a scull and mast maker; James Barnett, next door, a ships' chandler offering canvas, rope fend-offs, lamp glasses and oakum for both river and canal trade. Two of the three children have no shoes – a sign of abject poverty.

Right: 91-97 Three Colt Street, Limehouse, c1923

Three of the five weatherboarded houses shown in the Edwardian photographs on page 91 can be seen here in an advanced state of decay, the wooden gable wall supported by a single prop. Two are derelict, but the ground floor of the third is in use as a greengrocers with a pram inventively deployed to support an impromptu market stall.

Opposite: 9 Gainsborough Road, Hackney Wick, 29 May 1909
Pawnbrokers were a common sight across London and their regular use a way of life in the East End. Edwin Brigham was typical, offering short-term loans against items of value. The window is crammed with clocks, vases, watches and silver, whilst the crowd milling outside shows that there was no shortage of business.

Above: Aldermanbury Almshouses, 52-60 Phillip Street, Hackney, c1910
The endowment of almshouses was a favourite form of charitable bequest. For a lucky few, they offered a real alternative to the workhouse or the streets. Local tradition alleged that the curious house to the left of the picture was built with stone from old London Bridge. This was probably true as a stone tablet inside the party wall stated it was built in 1817 by Mr Malcott, who also built Old Bridge House, 54 Streatham Hill (demolished 1928) utilising stone from the bridge, hence the name.

Main picture: 215-223 Bow Road, Bow, 19 November 1909
A fine group of buildings of various periods just east of St Mary's Church. The houses to the extreme left and right still stand, but the remainder have been swept away, including the impressive, eight-bay Georgian façade to Anderson's, which was believed to have been erected for Lord Sheffield in 1612, close to the old Royal Palace at Bromley-by-Bow built six years earlier for James I.

Above: 217 Bow Road, Bow, 9 November 1905
The magnificent Jacobean ceiling on the first floor of Lord Sheffield's ancient mansion. By 1905 the entire neighbourhood had declined, engulfed by the remorseless spread of London and the development of the nearby Lea Valley into a cauldron of noxious industries. At the time of the photograph, the building was in use as a dormitory by the Workmen's Homes next door.

Opposite & right: The Old Farm House, Disney Place, Marshalsea Road, Borough, 17 February 1910

"There is probably no more picturesque building left standing in London-Over-the-Water than the ancient residence known as the Farm House" (*Daily Chronicle*, 9 January 1914).

The Old Farm House was a remarkable survival tucked away at the end of a cul-de-sac and may have been a remnant of a 16th century house built for the Earl of Suffolk. It fell into use as a doss-house and paupers of many parishes were farmed out here – hence the name. For a while it was the lodging of the Welsh tramp poet, W H Davies, who wrote and published *The Soul's Destroyer and other Poems* from here. Dickens knew it well. The brackets to the elaborate 17th century door canopy are still in place, but its roof has gone. The spectral figure of a young girl can be seen inside the doorway.

Right: As a common lodging house beds were crammed into every room. The first floor east room, shown here, retained its fine original panelling and chimney piece, crudely whitewashed with a single gas mantle suspended from the ceiling. A chamber pot can be glimpsed beneath the bed.

Above: The Old Farm House, Disney Place,
Marshalsea Road, 17 February 1910
The ground floor parlour used by the housekeeper is in marked contrast to
the spartan conditions in the communal bedrooms above. The furnishings,
piano and pictures suggest a reputable middle-class household.

Main picture: Moss's Alley, Bankside, 16 May 1912
View looking north from the junction with Ladd's Court – a bleak, harsh
world of hard unremitting grind with the mark of poverty stamped indelibly
both on the faces of the people and on the houses.

   To the left the chalk marks read 'Chocolate Club Held Here'. The child to
the right seems intent on throttling a kitten. His mother seems prematurely
old, but is probably less than 30.

Above: Ladd's Court, Bankside, 16 May 1912
The squalid mass of dingy streets and sunless alleys behind Bankside contained some of the worst housing in London and the highest concentrations of poverty – 68%. The large number of people gathered outside their homes bears witness to chronic overcrowding and high levels of deprivation. Frequently, tiny back to back dwellings like these contained more than one family in a single room.

Opposite: Taylor's Yard, Bankside, 16 May 1912
View from Moss's Alley into Taylor's Yard. Chronic poverty and overcrowding went hand in hand. Of the 24 people in the photograph, 14 are small children – all crammed into three mean dwellings at the end of a blind alley overshadowed by the walls of the adjacent sawmills.

Right: Moss's Alley, Bankside, 16 May 1912
Parts of Moss's Alley were less than 8ft wide, but provided access to a whole nest of small subsidiary courts and yards crammed with families categorised by Charles Booth in the lowest class as semi-criminal, along with occasional labourers and loafers, their children classified as street "arabs".

Opposite: Grange Walk, Bermondsey, c1905
Grange Walk stands on the site of Bermondsey Abbey, of which fragments still remain. The house to the right, which is occupied, has broken front windows – a hallmark of poverty. In the 18th century the brick houses with carved doorcases beyond would have been occupied by prosperous merchants, but as the area declined they fell to multiple occupation.

Above: 24-26 Jacob Street, Bermondsey, c1910
Timber houses were built in Bermondsey and Southwark using a ready supply of wood from nearby wharves, long after they were proscribed in the Building Act of 1707. These old 18th century houses with massive central chimney stacks were once part of the infamous rookery of Jacob's Island, the setting for Bill Sikes' death in *Oliver Twist*; but by 1910 the area was much changed. The houses seem well cared-for and the occupants relatively respectable.

Opposite: 92-101 Snowsfields, Bermondsey, 30 September 1943
This wartime view could have been taken 50 years earlier. Little has changed – dingy, soot-blackened frontages and an air of world-weary decrepitude characterised many of London's poorest districts. Surprisingly for wartime, Oxford Farm Dairy is well-stocked with canned produce.

Right: Brune Place, Newington Butts, Elephant & Castle, 26 November 1911
The cottages at the end of the court are marked with a plaque – Rose Court 1708 – but the remainder are later, 19th century terraces. Those to the left are more generous than most with small front yards for drying washing. The woman in the foreground is heavily pregnant, but all appear to be tired, worn out and depressed.

Opposite: 34 Albury Street, Deptford, 30 April 1911
A wonderfully evocative view of the nursery in the ground floor rear room. Note the wooden horse by the table and the copy of Goosey Gander on the mantelpiece.

Left: 242 Rotherhithe Street, 8 November 1911
An 18th century survivor sandwiched between two later buildings. The house is in poor condition, the windows broken and the weatherboarding held in place by straps. The sign next door offers 'Tea Outdoors at 1d Pint'.

Opposite: 48 Hoxton Square, 1921
View of the south side. Hoxton Square, built in the 1680s, was home to one of the first Dissenters' Academies. By 1902 it was synonymous with poverty, overcrowding and crime, characterised by Charles Booth as "the leading criminal quarter of London, and indeed of all England" – the home of the pickpocket, "whizzer" or "dip", and gangs of shoplifters or "hoisters". It is now one of London's coolest neighbourhoods, a centre for creative industries and nightlife.

Although bombed heavily, some of the original houses survived into the 1970s. Today only a handful remain.

Above: 209 Mare Street, Hackney, 30 May 1904
A fascinating glimpse of the first floor rear room of No. 209 with typical early 18th century square-edged panelling, a plain chimneypiece, butterfly hinges to the china cupboard, and religious tracts on the walls.

Opposite: 4 Philipots Almshouses, Philipots Path, Greenwich, c1910
Philipots Almshouses were built in 1694, and demolished for road widening in 1931. In this evocative view of the ground floor front room are all the common accoutrements of a simple Edwardian interior: a range in the fireplace, a piano and – the final touch – an aspidistra on the table. The picture of the Naval Review and framed sailor's portrait highlight the strong maritime links with the nearby Royal Naval Hospital.

Above: Moneyer Street, Hoxton, 1931

As early as the 17th century Hoxton was renowned for its market and nursery gardens, and related trades continued well into the 20th century. Columbia Road market is still a mecca for gardeners and enthusiasts.

View showing the north end with carts piled high with plants, shrubs and saplings.

Opposite: Lynedoch Street, Shoreditch, July 1920

The City of Dreadful Monotony. Each house shoulder to shoulder with its neighbour, two storeys high and 18ft wide; street after street of grimy buildings against a slate-coloured sky. Yet beneath the drab exterior lay vibrant working class communities offering each other help and support in times of acute need.

Opposite: Waterloo Road, c1930
Dilapidated stucco buildings at the junction of Waterloo Road and The Cut.

Above: Swedenborg Square, Stepney, 19 August 1945
Swedenborg Square was one of the East End's most historic places occupied for generations by mariners and seafaring families. The houses with raised basements and elegant Doric doorcases were highly unusual. By 1945 they were in poor condition, and are shown here with their pilasters stripped, prior to demolition.

Above: 26 Steward Street, Stepney, 20 November 1944
As a result of extensive damage during the Blitz, in many districts it was difficult to find a single house with unbroken windows. London exuded hardship, poverty and desolation, which fuelled idealistic concepts of town planning which in turn catastrophically destroyed more of London's unique historic neighbourhoods than the Luftwaffe did.

Opposite: 3 Upper Street, Islington, 30 May 1944
An evocative snapshot of tired wartime London with vitrolite fascias to the shopfronts and dilapidated frontages to the upper floor.

CHANGE

"Nothing endures, but change"
(Heraclitus)

London was the first great metropolis of the modern age. In 1800 it was a major European capital of one million people. By 1911 it was the largest city in the world – greater than the combined populations of Paris, Berlin, St Petersburg and Moscow. This phenomenal expansion was unique, creating a city unlike any other with its own distinctive form and character. As London expanded outwards from its twin centres in the City of London and Westminster, whole districts were laid out to a common pattern by surveyors using the Imperial system of measures and proportion. Everything deployed in the construction of public spaces, houses and their internal furnishings derived from the human form, which accounts for the remarkable unity and visual cohesion of Georgian and Victorian London (p114).

One of the unique characteristics of this city was, and still remains, the London square. Terraces of individual houses, each subordinated to the wider composition, were set around communal gardens enclosed by railings for the enjoyment of surrounding residents. By 1900 there were over 460 across the capital. As well as providing much needed oases of green space, they created a highly distinctive urban grain which imparted a unity to the city as a whole and linked the wealthiest with the poorest neighbourhoods.

Much of the subsequent development of London led to the fragmentation of this unified whole – with the advent of the railways, road widening, metropolitan improvements and the construction of much larger buildings on aggregated plots for a whole variety of new uses. Nevertheless, a great deal of this urban backcloth still remains, in areas like Islington, Bloomsbury, Hackney, Camberwell and Lambeth.

With the development of public transport, London embraced, and later subsumed, outlying villages, as low density suburbs spread inexorably across the Home Counties. As a result many of London's urban villages retain much older cores.

The distinctive character of the Victorian city was castigated by many as remorselessly monotonous. Dickens lamented its unremitting shabbiness. By 1900 London was an extraordinary kaleidoscope of districts with a constantly shifting social geography as areas declined, prospered or were redeveloped with bewildering rapidity – a process which continues to this day. Older domestic buildings and areas were swept away as large swathes of London were transformed into a great commercial and Imperial capital.

In Whitehall, the government precinct was transformed as the great offices of state in old 17th and 18th century houses gave way to a magnificent new generation of government palaces (p143). The very heart of ceremonial London was remodelled to reflect the Imperial zeitgeist. In 1912 Sir Aston Webb completed its reconfiguration with a spectacular example of monumental axial planning from Trafalgar Square through the new Admiralty Arch (pp262-263) to a new rond-point at the Victoria Memorial and on to Hyde Park Corner. The entire east front of Buckingham Palace was refaced in just three months, replacing Edward Blore's lacklustre façade.

The momentum of civic improvement continued relentlessly. The Holborn to Strand improvement scheme, which had been under discussion for over 60 years, was the largest single clearance of buildings since the Great Fire, overseen by the newly-founded London County Council which specified height limitations and a classical style (pp237, 239). Beneath Kingsway a modern tram tunnel was constructed entered from beneath Waterloo Bridge and emerging at Theobalds Road (pp254-255).

Further west the reconstruction of Nash's Regent Street began simultaneously (pp272-281). The gradual accretion of signs, fascias, awnings, royal warrants and blown coats of paint over the original bare Roman cement finishes so impaired the original composition that many welcomed redevelopment. The authorities simply specified fire-resisting construction, Portland stone, a uniform height of 60ft to the cornice, and two roof storeys at a 75 degree pitch in green Westmoreland slate, but completion took almost 30 years.

In the City and West End large swathes of central London were rebuilt in Edwardian Beaux Arts style in a magnificent expression of civic pride and Imperial self-confidence. In the City new citadels were raised for banking, shipping and insurance. Across the capital palatial new buildings arose which expressed the political and commercial might of the British Empire (p206 and pp214-215).

By 1939 the population of London was 8.2 million – well ahead of New York with 6.93 million – the seat of the monarchy, the government and the judiciary. It was widely acknowledged to be the finest city in the world, but it was also a shockingly vulnerable target on the brink of catastrophe and massive unimaginable change during the Second World War.

Left: Unilever House under construction, 1 August 1930
View towards Blackfriars station from Tudor Street.

Opposite: Sir Paul Pindar's house, Bishopsgate, c1885

As a boy, Sir Paul Pindar was apprenticed to a London merchant, who employed him as a factor in Italy where he made his fortune, later becoming British ambassador to Turkey. On his return to London in the early 1600s, he built this splendid mansion with an elaborately-carved oak frontage, which can be seen here in use as a tavern, just prior to its demolition for the Great Eastern Railway in 1890. The frontage was dismantled and re-erected at the Victoria & Albert Museum; a tangible indication of growing antiquarian interest in London's vanishing past.

Left: Bartholomew Close, Cloth Fair, 1906

Weatherboarded timber-framed house with a grocer's shop on the ground floor. The arrival of the photographer was an occasion of considerable local curiosity. Hats were a mark of respectability; note the variety of headgear – top hats, bowlers and cloth caps are worn by men and boys of all ages.

Opposite: Aylesbury Place, Clerkenwell, 19 October 1912
The houses on the east side of Jerusalem Passage have been cleared revealing the remains of the mediaeval Hall of the Priory of St John of Jerusalem in the foreground. Around the mediaeval basement walls can be seen dressed stone, masonry and pipework of great archaeological value which is being discarded. The 18th century houses in the background on the west side of Jerusalem Passage still exist.

Left: 11 St John's Square, Clerkenwell, 30 January 1907
In this oblique view the earlier 17th century building can be seen clearly behind the skin of the later front façade. The posters are of particular interest. The *Weekly Dispatch* leads with the "The Great Tichborne Mystery" and *Lloyds News* with "The Jamaica Earthquake" for its Sunday edition on 20 January.

Right: 10-11 Norton Folgate, Spitalfields, 25 March 1909

The Golden Eagle was a dispensing chemist founded in 1750 with a delightful double-bowed shop front of about 1780, a railed stall board and brass cill bands engraved with the names of the store – Peter Jones, similar to the old Fribourg & Treyer shopfront which still survives in Haymarket. The traditional apothecaries' jars can be seen in the left-hand window. No. 10 was occupied continuously by lead and glass merchants from 1809 until the 20th century.

Opposite: 1-2 Little Prescot Street, Tower, 14 December 1906

Little Prescot Street shortly before clearance in 1907 for the widening and extension of Mansell Street to meet Tower Bridge Approach. O'Connell's Coffee and Dining Rooms in the background catered for carmen serving the surrounding goods depots. A rasher and two eggs could be had for 4d.

HOLLAND & HANNEN
AND
CUBITTS LTD

Opposite: Unilever House site, New Bridge Street, Blackfriars, 12 September 1930

View looking south towards Victoria Embankment showing Unilever House under construction with the City of London school 1881-82 to the right. Built on the site of Henry VIII's Bridewell Palace, later prison, Unilever House by J Lomax-Simpson was one of the most lavish architectural expressions of British commercial power in the inter-war period dominating the view across Blackfriars Bridge.

Right: Unilever House site, New Bridge Street, 17 July 1930

View from Tudor Street east towards New Bridge Street showing the demolition of the well-known De Keyser's Royal Hotel, which unearthed mediaeval brick arches from the old Bridewell prison.

Left: Catherine Court, Tower, 25 January 1913
Catherine Court was a narrow court of early Georgian houses between Seething Lane and Trinity Square enclosed at each end by wrought iron gates. The plaque is dated 1725. The entire street block was cleared for the sumptuous new Port of London Authority building by Sir Edwin Cooper in 1912, although construction was interrupted by the First World War, and it was not completed until 1932. The poster on the wall advertises the sale of antique fixtures and fittings from the houses. The fine carved Corinthian porch to the double-fronted house on the right was sold for £145, the equivalent of £7,500 today.

Opposite: Savage Gardens, Tower, 20 June 1913
View looking north from Trinity Square with the side of Trinity House to the right. Note the angled mirror to reflect light into the ground floor windows of the flank elevation of Trinity House.

Left: Trinity House, Trinity Square, 16 April 1941

Trinity House, the General Lighthouse Authority for England and Wales, commissioned its existing headquarters from Samuel Wyatt in 1793; the foundation stone was laid by William Pitt, the Master of the Corporation. Completely gutted by bombing in 1941, the headquarters were rebuilt by Sir Albert Richardson behind the surviving façades in 1953. The extent of wartime damage can be seen clearly.

Opposite: 8 Bow Churchyard, Cheapside, 30 August 1908

This splendid 17th century house stood next to St Mary-le-Bow, Cheapside. The old Crown glass can be seen clearly in the original flush-framed sash windows. To the left, a narrow passage leads through into Bow Lane. The structure on the footway is probably a watchman's hut.

Opposite & above: Christ's Hospital, Newgate Street, c1906
Christ's Hospital occupied a large area between St Bartholomew's Hospital and King Edward Street. Founded in 1552 on the site of the old Greyfriars Monastery, it was demolished amid great public outcry in 1908. This view shows the austere arcaded 18th century elevation of the writing school in the western courtyard with earlier late 17th century masters' buildings adjacent.

Above: A haunting view of the rear elevation of the south range of the 17th century school buildings designed by Sir Christopher Wren showing the burial ground of Christ Church, Newgate Street in the foreground with the church in the distance.

Opposite & above: Christ's Hospital, Newgate Street, c1906
The Court Room by Sir Christopher Wren with its fine vaulted ceiling and fluted Corinthian screen.

Above: A melancholy view of the band room in the attic over the fourth floor.

Left: Christ's Hospital, Newgate Street, 20 June 1908
View looking north-west during demolition of the main hall showing the chalk walls of the earlier mediaeval Greyfriars monastery. In the distance are the tower and rear of the newly-completed outpatients block of St Bartholomew's Hospital by l'Anson 1903-07.

Main picture: General Post Office, St Martin's-Le-Grand, 26 July 1911
Designed by Sir Robert Smirke and opened in 1829, the General Post Office was one of the most elegant buildings in London with a grand Greek Revival frontage. A new GPO building was opened on the site of Christ's Hospital in King Edward Street immediately to the west in the same year – 1911– that Smirke's landmark was demolished. In the foreground are the railings and steps to a subterranean public convenience proclaimed by an elaborate lamp column over a cast-iron ventilator.

Above: St Paul's Churchyard, 21 June 1912
East elevation from No. 7 Cheapside to Watling Street. View looking south towards the spire of St Augustine's Church. Sorosis Shoes has a fine sinuous Art Nouveau shopfront and lettering.

Main picture: Junction of Old Change and Watling Street, c1905
The south-east corner of St Paul's Churchyard viewed from the west with Cannon Street to the right and an elegant semi-circular block of Italianate offices in the foreground. The entire area was earmarked for clearance for St Paul's Bridge, a new Thames crossing, which was eventually abandoned. St Augustine Church (1680-83 by Wren) was destroyed in the Second World War, but rebuilt around surviving remnants as part of St Paul's Choir School.

Opposite: 32-34 Tower Hill, c1920
This once elegant late 18th century building stood north-east of the Tower with Eastminster (formerly King Street) beyond to the left. The flank elevation and box cornice of No. 1 Eastminster are clearly visible. Two elegant young women can be seen outside the tobacconist's to the right.

Left: 1-3 Eastminster, Tower Hamlets, 22 November 1920
A remarkable survival of a short row of late 17th century houses retaining their original bracketed timber box gutters, flush-framed sashes and steeply-pitched clay tile roofs. The iron bollards mark the boundary between the City of London and Tower Hamlets.

Opposite: The Black Bull Inn, Holborn, 8 April 1904

"Many a mournful procession passed its doors … coming up the 'Heavy Hill' on its way from Newgate or the Tower to the gallows at Tyburn."

Situated next to The Old Bell, the Black Bull was another well-known coaching inn. It was here that Sarah Gamp and Betsey Prig nursed Mr Lewsome in Dickens' *Martin Chuzzlewit*. The figure of the bull over the main entrance was modelled for William Lockwood, the inventor of Portland cement. On demolition for the new Gamages Department store, it was relocated to the offices of Sir William Bull MP in King Street, Hammersmith.

Right: The Old Bell Tavern & Hotel, Holborn, c1897

The frontage of The Old Bell dated from 1720, but the weatherboarded, galleried portion at the rear, where Shakespeare is alleged to have conducted one of his plays, was built in 1521. Dickens and Thackeray were both regulars. On the fascia to the right is a row of bells for summoning chambermaids, ostlers and staff. The site was redeveloped for the Prudential Assurance Co. in 1899, now the headquarters of English Heritage.

Left: 116-117 Theobald's Road, Holborn, 19 December 1910
The last of the old coaching inns rendered redundant by the railways and omnibuses of the new age as motorised transport displaced the horse. Here Bailey's covered vans can be seen in the foreground beneath the timber galleries to the courtyard.

Opposite: 85-87 Fetter Lane, 21 July 1908
A surviving group of 17th century, timber-framed houses at the north end of Chancery Lane. The gabled building in the background, a fine Edwardian Art Nouveau composition by the architects Treadwell and Martin, still remains (see p112). In the distance, the façade of the new Gamages department store can just be glimpsed.

Opposite & right: Clifford's Inn, Chancery Lane, 1903
Named after Robert de Clifford, who was granted the property by Edward II, an independent Inn was established by law students in 1345 and affiliated to the Inner Temple. The entire Inn was sold in 1903, when these photographs were taken, but it remained occupied until its demolition in 1935. Only the gateway survives. This view shows the Old Hall with its curious Gothic tower and cupola.

Right: The elegant young woman is probably the secretary of the South American Missionary Society that occupied the first floor of this range, which was built in 1682. Note the huge York stone slabs, cobbles and limestone setts to the courtyard.

Opposite: New Inn Passage, Aldwych, 11 June 1906
View along New Inn Passage from Houghton Street. To the left is a Girls' Infants School, which explains the large numbers of children around the entrance to the corner shop, which advertises Bovril, Old Chums Tobacco, Champions Mustard and R Whites Lemonade.

Above: St Clement Danes Church, Strand, 12 July 1906
View looking east from Newcastle Street showing the clearance of buildings by the LCC for the Holborn–Strand improvement scheme. The site in the foreground is now occupied by Australia House. The steeple of St Bride's, Fleet Street and the ethereal outline of St Paul's can be seen shimmering in the background haze.

Opposite: Strand, 22 May 1901

The east end of St Mary-le-Strand at the junction with Newcastle Street. The cart in the background is delivering large rolls of newspaper. Note the shoeshine boy, the colossal iron and glass lantern and exuberant display to The Lion public house on the corner.

Right: 321, 320 Strand, 11 June 1906

The north side of the Strand outside the west end of St Mary-le-Strand. Public drinking fountains were often the only available source of fresh drinking water, while horse troughs erected by the Metropolitan Drinking Fountain and Cattle Trough Association were the filling stations of their day. The elegant fountain seen here, modelled on the Choragic monument of Lysicrates in Athens, was re-erected at Wimbledon Common, where it survives.

Above: North side of Wych Street looking east, 11 June 1906
The Shakespeare Head boasts a magnificent cut glass ornamental gas lantern typical of the period. Martin Lemon, the editor of *Punch* was once the proprietor. It was also the meeting place of 'The Owls' – "a little quoting, quipping, quaffing club". Note the elegant Georgian shopfront to the left with bracketed, canted bays.

Opposite: 38-48 Wych Street, 5 July 1901
"There still remains some picturesque old patchwork buildings in and around Wych Street, Holywell Street and Drury Lane. Their picturesqueness largely relies on the varied and uncertain angles of tottering timbers, and the promiscuous arrangement of windows which protrude and overhang the little shops … Staircases lead to dingy rooms with hilly floors and blackened beams, running at all angles, drooping and groaning under the mingled weight of years and heavy tread" (*Pall Mall Gazette*, 17 October 1889).
This well-known group of Jacobean survivors stood on the south side of Wych Street, but were swept away for the Holborn–Strand scheme.

Left: Wych Street, 21 June 1901
View of the east end with the north side of St Clement Danes church in the middle distance and Fleet Street beyond. The timber-framed flank elevation of the Rising Sun public house is to the right, next to which is Constantine and Jackson, Surgical Rubber Stores. Note the pub lantern to the left with curved cut glass faces and a bulbous base suspended from a magnificent scrolled iron bracket.

Opposite: Junction of Wych Street and Holywell Street, c1910
The Rising Sun was a fine Elizabethan tavern, at the junction with Holywell Street. In the bar was a glass case containing a bone of Sir Thomas Armstrong who was hanged, drawn and quartered without trial for suspicion of involvement in the Rye House Plot, 1683. One of his quarters was fixed over Temple Bar. Dislodged in a high wind, it was brought to the pub as "everlasting testimony to the lawlessness of the law". The frontage facing St Clement Danes boasts a brash new illuminated sign for "Dewars Whisky" obscuring the old Elizabethan structure behind, but the gabled roof and railed parapet of its neighbour bear witness to its early origins. The suspended lantern is a veritable leviathan.

Main picture & right: Holywell Street, Strand, 11 June 1906
View looking east with a fine old timber-framed house to the right. In spite of its notorious reputation for pornography, and its constriction of traffic along the Strand, Holywell Street was a place of immense character. The prints outside the shop in the middle distance (right) seem to be arousing great interest.

The complete absence of women in both photographs is hardly surprising, given the street's raffish reputation as a centre for lewd prints and photographs.

Opposite: Craven Buildings, Strand, 11 June 1906
Craven Buildings were erected in 1723 on part of the grounds of Craven House. At the end of
the street was once a fresco of the Earl of Craven in armour, which was plastered over around
1813, but the panelled wall can be seen clearly in the distance. The undertaker's lantern on the
extreme left advertises 'Funerals to Suit all Classes'.

Above: Drury Lane, Strand, 11 June 1906
The junction of Drury Lane and Wych Street with Drury Court off to the right and St Mary
le-Strand beyond. A pervasive miasma of smoke from thousands of coal fires contaminated
the air and coated buildings in thick black grime. Winter fogs, known as London "particular"
or "pea-soupers", were commonplace.

Opposite: Vere Street, Aldwych, 11 June 1906
This early 18th century corner building was formerly The Blackmoor public house, which gave its name to Blackmoor Street, a continuation of Clare Street. The plaque on the splayed corner depicts two negroes' heads, the initials S.W.M. and the date 1715.

Above: Blackmoor Street, Aldwych, 9 October 1902
Blackmoor Street was a narrow thoroughfare linking Drury Lane with Clare Street. A side entrance to Clare Court can be seen to the left. The setted road surface with twin cart tracks was only wide enough for a single vehicle.

Left: Drury Court, Strand, 11 June 1906

Drury Court linked Drury Lane with the Strand. The portico of St Mary-le-Strand can be seen in the distance. To the left is Ben Jewell, a Rags, Bones and Fat merchant. The gap site next door shows the truncated timbers and laths of a timber-framed house. The poster for the Duke of York's Theatre trails "The Girl from Up There".

Opposite: Newcastle Street, Strand, 11 June 1906

The east side of Newcastle Street between Wych Street and the Strand. The area was renowned for its dealers in second-hand furniture, bedding and old clothes. The Globe Theatre, which held 1500 people, had its pit and stage underground, the dress circle and boxes being level with Newcastle Street. Another entrance in Wych Street provided access to the gallery and royal box. The large poster between the second floor windows of the corner building advertises the Earl's Court Military Exhibition complete with the British lion, Union Jacks and pith-helmeted soldier.

Above: Denzell Street, Aldwych, c1906

The junction of Denzell Street and Stanhope Street. The pub advertises a glass of gin for 4d. On the opposite corner lies the pawnbrokers, which has relocated prior to demolition. Beyond Finch & Co on the right is the mixed Parochial School.

Opposite: Wesleyan Chapel, Great Queen Street, 22 May 1906

Opened in 1817, the elegant Ionic portico of Welsh stone was added in 1840 beneath the fine tripartite north window. The chapel was demolished in 1910.

Opposite: Bush House, Aldwych, c1932
Brave new world. View of Bush House at the
centre of the great axial vista south from Kingsway,
but prior to the completion of its wings. In the
distant haze beyond is the façade of Somerset
House. The Holborn to Strand improvements
incorporated an underground tramway tunnel,
opened in 1906, the entrance to which can be seen
in the foreground.

Right: Southampton Row, Holborn, c1906
A single-decker tram emerging from the tram
tunnel in Southampton Row before it was
deepened to take double-decker trams in 1930-31.
Beyond are the flank elevations of Carlisle House
and Baptist Church House. To the extreme left, the
Central School of Arts & Crafts, designed by the
LCC Architects Department under W E Riley, is in
the course of construction.

Right: Trafalgar Square, 31 July 1896
Panoramic view of Charing Cross. Le Sueur's famous statue of Charles I can be seen in the middle distance. Beyond the horse-drawn omnibus are the buildings at Charing Cross, soon to be removed for the creation of Mall Approach and Admiralty Arch.

Left: Trafalgar Square, 31 July 1896
Panoramic view from the National Gallery looking south with the statue of General Sir Charles Napier to the right. In the background is a group of horse-drawn omnibuses.

Opposite: Trafalgar Square, 31 July 1896

Early morning view taken at 8.30am looking west from the corner of Morley's Hotel on the east side of the square. Note the shoeshine equipment at the pavement's edge. Behind the genteel group to the right is the statue of Major General Sir Henry Havelock, the hero of the relief of Lucknow. Such was the esteem in which he was held that on his death from exhaustion, during the Indian Mutiny, the lights of all the ships in New York Harbour were dimmed on news of his passing. The posters announce the marriage between Prince Charles of Denmark and Princess Maud of Wales in the private chapel at Buckingham Palace on 22 July. In the distance behind the plinth of Nelson's Column is an Electric Time Signal Ball.

Above: Trafalgar Square, c1890

Horse-drawn London. View looking east on the south side towards Grand Buildings with Morley's Hotel to the left. A hexagonal Penfold pillar box can be seen on the traffic island.

Left: Admiralty Arch, Mall Approach, 21 November 1910

Admiralty Arch in the process of completion. Sir Aston Webb's remodelling of the Mall, Buckingham Palace and the completion of the Queen Victoria Memorial was one of the finest examples of grand axial planning in Europe, transforming the old ceremonial heart of London into a magnificent new Imperial capital.

Opposite: Spring Gardens Chapel, 1903
St Matthew's Chapel was built in 1731
on an irregular plot and functioned until
1885 when it was used as a storehouse for
Admiralty records. It was part of a compulsory
purchase by the Commissioners of Works and
demolished in 1903 for the replanning of the
Mall and Admiralty Arch.

Left: Spring Gardens Chapel, 1903
Assorted items of furniture awaiting disposal
prior to demolition including, bizarrely, a
penny-farthing bicycle.

Above: Westminster Hospital, Broad Sanctuary, c1910

Westminster Hospital stood opposite the Abbey and opened for patients in 1834. It was designed by W and H W Inwood between 1831-34 in a Tudor Gothic style and extended in the later 19th century. Originally it had room for over 100 patients, but only two baths, and drained into a cesspool. The hospital moved to Horseferry Road in 1939, but the building survived until 1951. The Queen Elizabeth II Conference Centre was built on the site between 1981-86.

Opposite: St George's Hospital, Hyde Park Corner, c1910

A view of St George's Hospital taken from the first floor of Apsley House, popularly known as No. 1 London. Built between 1827-33 in neo-Greek style to the designs of William Wilkins, the great central portico is based on the Choragic monument of Thrasyllus. The hospital closed in 1980. After standing vacant as one of London's most prominent buildings at risk for about 10 years, in 1991 it was converted into the exclusive Lanesborough Hotel.

**Left: Waterloo Place,
St James's, c1907**
A remarkable view of Waterloo
Place looking north to Piccadilly
Circus showing Nash's original
buildings with the Guards
Crimea Memorial in the
foreground and a complete
absence of traffic.

VAN RAALTE

VAN RAALTE & SONS

2

Drink **perrier** Water.

AMERY & LOADER.

BOV
PRO

BOTTLED BY SO

MELLIN'S FOOD

MELLIN'S EMULSION

Mellins Food

RESTAURANT

F.A. STIFF & Cº ESTATE AGENTS

S.VAN RAALTE & SONS

MELLIN'S PHARMACY 48

PRESCRIPTIONS PREPARED
MELLIN'S FOOD DEPOT

CAFÉ MONICO.

CAFÉ MONICO

CAFÉ MONICO

CAFÉ MONICO   INTERNATIONAL HALL

44   44

Regent Sᵗ

PLIM.   SHIRTS   C. FITS   GLOVES   CRAVATS   44

SAQUI & LAWRENCE
SILVERSMITHS   OPTICIANS

SAQUI & LAWRENCE

JEWELLERS & GOLDSMITHS   SAQUI & LAWRENCE   DIAMOND MERCHANTS

Opposite: 44-48 Regent Street, 1910
Elaborate advertising attached to
prominent buildings was a hallmark
of the Victorian city, but in the 1890s
illuminated lettering began to be
introduced. By 1910 it was well-
established on the north-east corner of
Piccadilly Circus in spite of attempts
by the London County Council to
resist it. The first illuminated sign
above fascia level was probably Mellins
Pharmacy at No. 48, but it was almost
certainly unauthorised. The Crown
Estate Commissioners resisted similar
displays on the Criterion, Swan &
Edgar and other adjacent buildings
under their control through strict
covenants.

**Right: Shaftesbury Memorial
Fountain, Piccadilly Circus, 1909**
An atmospheric picture of the
Shaftesbury Memorial Fountain (1886-
93) by Alfred Gilbert, crowned by the
winged figure of Anteros; the first use
of aluminium on a large-scale English
monument. It rapidly became a
London icon and the focus for flower-
sellers and newspaper boys.

Left: Regent Street, c1910
Only once has a great plan
for London been conceived
and completed. The great
metropolitan improvements of
the Regency created a whole new
spine through the centre of the
West End and triggered a wave
of northward expansion. Built as
a personal speculation by John
Nash between 1818-19, originally
the Quadrant had continuous
Doric colonnades running at
street level in a great curve from
the projecting pavilions; the latter
remained but the colonnades
were removed in 1848 to improve
daylight and discourage vice.
View showing the Quadrant
c1910 prior to reconstruction.
In the distance is a new office
building breaking Nash's carefully
orchestrated parapet line.

Left: 83-99 Regent Street, 4 August 1914
There is little evidence that this was taken on the day Britain declared war on Germany. Life appears to continue as normal with the sandwich-boards promoting seaweed baths in Great Portland Street. To the left is the abrupt end of Norman Shaw's Piccadilly Hotel which triggered the complete reconstruction of the remainder of Regent Street as the leases progressively expired. A branch of the Parisian Samaritaine department store proves a popular draw. Above is a sign for Hillier Parker, which remains one of London's leading estate agents.

Left: 153-167 Regent Street, 8 August 1912
View of the west side south of New Burlington Street showing the elaborate ironwork over Hudson Bay House, the International Fur Store, and a battery of royal warrants over shopfronts. Truth being sold by the news vendor highlights 'Robber Devils of Peru' above a reference to the *Titanic* disaster four months earlier.

Left: 154-142 Regent Street, 1913
Originally Liberty's store stood on the east side of Regent Street south of the junction with Beak Street which can be seen to the left, before it relocated further north in the early 1920s. The paired fluted Corinthian columns are embellished with two grand royal warrants. Around the corner in Beak Street, the Liberty's clock stands frozen in time at 4pm.

Above: 170-160 Regent Street, 4 March 1913

Robinson & Cleaver's department store in the throes of demolition. This striking block was designed by Sir John Soane and completed in 1821 in his characteristic style with simple incised pilasters. The much altered central pavilion is crowned by a figure of Mercury flanked by eagles. To the north a run of ladders is fixed to a huge flagpole.

Opposite: 144-122 Regent Street, 10 October 1913

The southern half of the Liberty's terrace shown on pages 278-279. Sainsbury's is at No. 136. The flank elevation at the extreme right shows the change in height and scale of the new development which progressively replaced Nash's original buildings.

Above: 52 Wardour Street, Soho, c1910
This elegant Regency shop front with shallow bays to each frontage stood on the corner of Wardour Street and Old Compton Street until its demolition in the 1920s. Old apothecaries jars can be seen in the windows.

Main picture: 34-39 Lisle Street, Soho, 26 July 1910
A fine terrace of late 18th century houses with a good run of contemporary shopfronts and a wealth of detail. The newsagents to the left has an enamel sign for the National Telephone Company to advertise a public telephone prior to the introduction of street kiosks. The placard for the *Mirror* leads with 'Women Watch Liners for Dr Crippen'. A similar terrace still survives on the north side now used by the Chinese community as shops and restaurants.

Above: Euston Road, King's Cross, 1928
A murky view of the south side at the junction with Tonbridge Street with a cleared site
awaiting sale and development, later the location for the new St Pancras Town Hall, built
on the site between 1934-37 to the designs of A J Thomas, who worked with Lutyens.
The site hoardings are enriched with an evocative display of period advertisements.

Opposite: Cromer Street, King's Cross, January 1928
View of the south side at the west end showing a builders' yard eccentrically embellished
with items of architectural salvage. To the right is the front of an Albion van.

Opposite: Euston Arch, January 1948
Looking tired and shabby in the aftermath of the Second World War, the Euston Arch was an heroic
monument to Britain's railway age. This huge Greek Doric propylaeum, built in 1838 to the design of Philip
Hardwick, rose over 70ft to form a gigantic gateway to Euston, the first mainline terminus in a capital city
anywhere in the world. Its demolition in 1962 triggered a public outcry which did much to boost the growth
of the conservation movement and popular reaction against the institutional philistinism which characterised
the post-war period.

Above: 154 Albany Street, St Pancras, 1929
This elegant stucco range was designed by John Nash in 1818 as the Army Ophthalmic Hospital, but by 1929
it had been converted into a mineral water factory. Immediately beyond is the steeple of Christ Church, 1837-
39 by James Pennethorne. Note the fine embossed cast iron utility cabinet to the right.

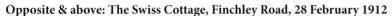

Opposite & above: The Swiss Cottage, Finchley Road, 28 February 1912
Built as an inn in the 1840s, The Swiss Cottage public house became a local landmark and gave its name to the entire district as it developed. The main buildings, which still survive, can be seen behind the brick cottages in the foreground. Finchley Road is to the right leading towards St John's Wood. To the left is Avenue Road with a granite drinking fountain in the foreground.

Above: The kitchen of the public house with a display of china and cooking utensils under the watchful eye of the cook and her cat at 4.15 in the afternoon.

Opposite: Tower Bridge, c1893

The need for a new river crossing was identified as early as 1879. Authorised by an Act of Parliament in 1885, it was designed by the City Corporation architect, Sir Horace Jones and the engineer, John Wolfe Barry as a bascule bridge to allow the passage of large ships into the Pool of London. The Act stipulated a clear span of 200ft, a height of 135ft and the use of the Gothic style to harmonise with the Tower of London. Tower Bridge opened in 1894 and rapidly became a London icon. The new Tower Bridge Approach Road required extensive demolition on the north bank.

The iron frame and upper level walkway can be seen here rising from the great stone bastions sunk into the river.

Above: St Olave's Churchyard, Tooley Street, c1910

Rebuilt in 1740 on the site of an earlier 12th century church, St Olave's stood just south-east of London Bridge. After a catastrophic waterfront fire in August 1843, the church was restored, only to be pulled down in 1926 to make way for St Olaf House. The churchyard with a number of chest tombs stood between the side of the church and the river. In this melancholic view, London Bridge can be seen dimly through the chill river fog.

Opposite: Mayflower Street, Rotherhithe, 16 May 1914
Mayflower Street (formerly Princes Street) was built in 1721-23 as grand houses with a variety of plan forms for sea captains and merchants. Once a gated street, it fell on hard times and by 1914 was in multiple occupation as lodging houses. Much of the street survived the war, but what remained was swept away in the mid-1950s.

Above: 298-312 Rotherhithe Street, 8 November 1911
An atmospheric view of Rotherhithe Street with St Paul's Lane entering from the right in the middle distance. William Corney's stores has a fine shallow, double-bowed shopfront. Beyond are late 17th century timber-framed houses with weatherboarded walls.

Above: 180 Meeting House Lane, Peckham, 21 January 1910

An interesting row of 17th century cottages. The plaque records that the house to the right was the original Meeting House of William Penn, the Quaker and founder of Pennsylvania. In 1947 The Society of Friends denied the statement. To the extreme left, next to G Williams, Removals by Pantechnicons and Large Covered Vans, is a coal and coke merchant. The placards are aimed at women: *Weldon's Ladies Journal* has 'Seven Patterns for February', while the *Daily Telegraph* offers 'Greek Dances and Dress for Modern Women'.

Opposite: Homestall Farm, Peckham Rye, 11 July 1908

A rustic idyll in the heart of Peckham. Enclosed by 150 year old elm trees, Homestall Farm was an old 17th century weatherboarded farmhouse with moss-grown, tiled roofs which was acquired by the LCC in 1894 for an extension to Peckham Rye Park to ease overcrowding in holidays. It was demolished in August 1908.

Left: The Earl Grey, Straightsmouth, Greenwich, 17 January 1913

A once-fine 18th century merchant's house with an elegant timber doorcase in use as a public house. It was not uncommon for ordinary domestic buildings to be used as public houses. Note the display of enamel advertisements and the large raking shore to the front wall. The General Dealer to the extreme right offers Best Prices for Old Iron. The Shops Act required it to close at one o'clock on Mondays.

Opposite: 6-7 Nile Street, Woolwich, c1900

These picturesque timber-framed, 16th century cottages, in what was once called Hog Lane, formed part of a wider group of ancient buildings, which were partly demolished for the Free Ferry in 1887-88. To the left is the Ferry Eel and Pie House with an elegantly-attired proprietress in the doorway. To her left, the older woman wears widow's weeds as a mark of mourning. A poster offers New Palace Steamers to Southend, Margate, Ramsgate, Deal and Dover.

Opposite: Lambeth Bridge, 8 June 1896
Old Lambeth Bridge looking south from Millbank. Lambeth Palace and St Mary's, Lambeth can be seen to the left in the distance. The old narrow lattice-stiffened suspension bridge by P W Barlow was never successful and suffered from severe corrosion. A new Lambeth Bridge was completed in 1932, upstream of the old, by the LCC's engineer Sir George Humphreys. The buildings in the foreground were pulled down for ICI's Nobel House (1927-29) and Thames House (1929-30), by Sir Frank Baines, one of the last expressions of late Imperial classical planning.

Above: Chelsea Bridge, c1930
An evocative period photograph of Chelsea Bridge from the south approach. On the right, note the woman and child with perambulator; to their left is an LCC tram stop for the 32 to Lavender Hill and Clapham: the tram tracks stop abruptly here. At the left of the picture is a delivery van.

Opposite: The George, The Broadway, Hammersmith, 26 July 1910
Originally called The White Horse, behind the later stucco front The George public house was a
17th century tavern and booking office for coaches, with extensive stabling and coach houses at
the rear. To the left, one of the curved bays of the grand Royal Sussex Arms public house can be
seen embellished with a coat of arms, clock and foliated iron brackets to the pendant lanterns.
The buildings were demolished for road widening. A new public house, also called The George,
was built immediately behind in 1911. At the pavement edge is an iron horse trough.

Above: The Cock & Magpie, 170 King Street, Hammersmith, 26 July 1910
Another early coaching inn with stable yard and garden was The Cock & Magpie public house
in King Street, a long, low building set back from the street beneath an ancient tiled roof with a
covered skittle ground. It was demolished in 1919 for the Gospel Hall of the Kelly Mission.

Above: 2 Great Cumberland Place, Marylebone, November 1928
A demolished corner plot at the junction with Oxford Street with huge raking shores propping the adjacent houses. To the right are the offices of Dunkley Prams.

Opposite: 22–40 Great Cumberland Place, Marylebone, 1941
View of the east side showing the damage caused by enemy action. Surface street shelters can be seen on the semi-circular forecourt. Subsequently the terrace was restored.

Above: St James's, Piccadilly, 1941

Built by Wren between 1676-84 to serve the new development of St James's, then being laid out by Henry Jermyn, Earl of St Albans, the church was damaged severely on 10 October 1940 by high explosives and incendiaries and the Vicarage completely destroyed. After extensive restoration by Sir Albert Richardson, it was rededicated in June 1954 incorporating many original details which survived the bombing, including a Renatus Harris organ from Whitehall Palace and a 17th century reredos by Grinling Gibbons. A new spire designed by Richardson was added in 1968.

Opposite: St Paul's Cathedral, 15 April 1942

View of St Paul's Cathedral from Friday Street with the ruins of St Augustine's Watling Street in the foreground. The narrow lanes around Old Change seen on pages 35 & 226 were flattened in the bombing.

Above: Fore Street, 10 March 1941

The City in ruins. View from Wood Street looking east along Fore Street towards Moorgate.

Opposite: Panorama from Milk Street, 16 April 1942

Beacons of hope in a sea of rubble: to the left are the ruins of St Alban, Wood Street, by Wren 1682-87, which was destroyed on 29 December 1940. The tower survived and was restored in 1964. Twenty years later it was converted into residential accommodation. In the distance is the tower of St Giles, Cripplegate. To the right is St Mary, Aldermanbury, also by Wren, which contained the tomb of Judge Jeffreys. The ruins were dismantled and shipped to Fulton, Missouri, where the church was reconstructed painstakingly on the campus of Westminster College as a memorial to Sir Winston Churchill.

Opposite: Nelson Square, Southwark, 1940

View of the north side of Nelson Square (1804-18) showing taped up windows to mitigate the effects of bomb blast. Beside the first floor windows of the house on the left are outdoor bird cages, once a common sight in inner London. Much of Nelson Square survived the war, but later was replaced by dull post-war council flats by Southwark Council. Only a fragment of the original terraces (Nos. 44-47) survives.

Above: King Square, Finsbury, 2 February 1945

Idealistic post-war planning destroyed more of London's historic neighbourhoods than the Luftwaffe did. King Square survived the war, but tragically the buildings were cleared for uninspiring public housing by Finsbury Borough Council in the 1960s.

Above: Brooke House, Hackney, 4 April 1941

Brooke House was a remarkable mediaeval house with its first recorded orgins in the 1470s.
Later it was possessed by Henry Percy, Earl of Northumberland, Thomas Cromwell and various
members of the nobility, one of whom, Baron Hunsdon, built the long gallery between 1578-83.
From 1759-1940 it was used as a private mental asylum, until October 1940 when it was hit by a
high explosive bomb, which destroyed the northern courtyard, seen here, and wrecked the rest of
the house. In 1944 it was acquired by the LCC, but after further bomb damage, it was demolished
completely in 1954-55; a great loss of a fascinating and historic mediaeval survival.

Opposite: Columbia Market, Shoreditch, 24 July 1946

Columbia Market was a white elephant virtually from its inception. It was founded in 1869 by
Baroness Burdett Coutts at a cost of over £200,000 in a philanthropic attempt to provide an
open food market for the East End, but it was frustrated by a monopoly of local interests and
closed in 1885. After acquisition by the LCC in 1915, it was used as workshops until it was finally
demolished for public housing in 1958 – one of London's most grievous architectural losses. This
view shows the west range, with the magnificent clock tower beyond whose carillon chimed a
hymn tune every 15 minutes.

Main picture & above: Columbia Market, Shoreditch, 24 July 1946
Ebullient high Victorian Gothic architecture by an accomplished practitioner, Henry Darbishire, architect to Baroness Burdett Coutts: view from the school playground adjoining the market.

Above: View of the magnificent Market Hall and Flemish Gothic clocktower from the main gate with the skeletal iron frame for market stalls in the foreground.

413-415 Strand, 1914

This fine pair of 17th century houses situated next to the
Adelphi Theatre with three storey projecting timber bays
were typical of many which survived in the Strand until
the early 20th century.

PANORAMAS OF LOST LONDON

WORK, WEALTH, POVERTY & CHANGE

1870-1945

INDEX

Above: Prince Albert public house, Albert Road, North Woolwich, 21 March 1899

ACKNOWLEDGEMENTS

Many people helped with the production of *Panoramas of Lost London*. First I must thank Murray Mahon and all the staff at Transatlantic Press and, in particular, Greg Hill, who played a pivotal role in enlarging some of the best photographs from the archive, and who designed the hugely successful English Heritage exhibition at Kenwood.

Foremost amongst the English Heritage staff who provided their skill and support were Richard Dumville, and my peerless secretary, Sue Woods, who provided unstinting support throughout the whole production process. Cathy Power, Treve Rosoman and all the staff at Kenwood House made a vital contribution, while Samantha Johnson willingly took on the onerous task of taking highlights of the exhibition to City Hall for the Mayor's *Story of London Festival*.

I would also like to thank all the staff at the English Heritage National Monuments Record in Swindon for their unrivalled knowledge and assistance including Anna Eavis, Alyson Rogers and Katherine Bryson for their cheerful tolerance of my endless requests support and information.

Particular thanks are due to Stefan Dickers at the Bishopsgate Institute, staff at the London Metropolitan Archives and various local history libraries including Anne Wheeldon at Hammersmith and Fulham and Malcolm Barr-Hamilton at Tower Hamlets.

Finally, special mention must be made of Jane Davies whose enthusiasm for London's history knows no bounds and whose unfailing support has been instrumental in bringing this book to fruition.

THE PHOTOGRAPHS

With the exception of those listed below, all the photographs in this book were taken from the collection of the former Greater London Council Historic Buildings Division, which subsumed the print collection of its predecessor, the London County Council. On the abolition of the Greater London Council in 1984 the print collection was transferred to the London Region of English Heritage where it remains in daily use for reference purposes. The negatives are held by the London Metropolitan Archives. The illustrations in this book are protected by copyright and may only be reproduced by permission of English Heritage or the London Metropolitan Archives, depending on the source of the image.

English Heritage is also the repository of the National Monuments Record (NMR). This was formed in 1941 as the National Buildings Record for recording historic buildings threatened by enemy action during the Second World War. In 1963 it became part of the Royal Commission on the Historical Monuments of England, which merged with English Heritage in 1999. Based in Swindon, the NMR is the most comprehensive archive of the historic environment in Britain comprising over 10 million photographs, drawings, documents and reports.

The author gratefully thanks the following for providing additional illustrations:
National Monuments Record:
p17(Swifts, Smithfield Market); p54 (Floral Hall, Covent Garden); p72 (Pool of London); p73 (Shad Thames); p110 (National Provincial Bank); p124 (27 Berkeley Square); p126 (22 Arlington Street); p127 (22 Arlington Street); p135 (Slater's); p143 (Westminster Embankment); p158 (Boundary Street); p159 (Abingdon Buildings); p261 (Trafalgar Square) – reproduced by permission of English Heritage NMR
Bishopsgate Institute:
p109 (Drapers' Hall); p132 (Piccadilly Circus); p243 (Wych Street/Holywell Street); p245 (Holywell Street); p255 (Southampton Row) – reproduced by kind permission of the Bishopsgate Institute
Guildhall Library
p208 (Sir Paul Pindar's house)
London Borough of Hammersmith & Fulham
p99 (210 New King's Road)

BIBLIOGRAPHY

Ackroyd, Peter: *London: The Biography*, Chatto & Windus 2000

Betjeman, John: *Victorian & Edwardian London from Old Photographs*, Batsford 1970

Brindle, Steven with Grady, Damian: *Shot from Above: Aerial Aspects of London*, English Heritage 2007

Booth, Charles: *Life and Labour of the People in London*, Macmillan 1902

Bush, Graham: *Old London: photographed by Henry Dixon and A & J Bool for the Society of Photographing Relics of Old London*, Academy Editions 1975

Chancellor, E Beresford: *The Private Palaces of London*, Kegan Paul 1908

Chancellor, E Beresford: *The West End of Yesterday and Today*, The Architectural Press 1926

Clunn, Harold: *London Rebuilt*, John Murray 1927

Cooper, Nicholas: *The Opulent Eye*, Architectural Press 1976

Davidoff, Leonore: *The Best Circles*, Croom Helm 1973

Davies, Philip: *Troughs and Drinking Fountains*, Chatto & Windus 1989

Dickens, Charles: *The Uncommercial Traveller*, President 1890

Fishman, William J: *The Streets of East London*, Duckworth 1987

Gordon, Charles: *Old Time Aldwych, The Kingsway and Neighbourhood*, 1903

Guillery, Peter: *The Small House in 18th Century London*, English Heritage 2004

Harrison, Fraser: *The Dark Angel: Aspects of Victorian Sexuality*, Sheldon Press 1977

Hibbert, Christopher: *London*, Longmans, Green & Co 1969

Hobhouse, Hermione: *Lost London: A Century of Demolition and Decay*, Macmillan 1971

Howgego, James L: *Victorian & Edwardian City of London from Old Photographs*, Batsford 1977

Information, Ministry of: *What Britain Has Done 1939-45*, 1945

London, Jack: *The People of the Abyss*, London, 1903

Mearns, Andrew: *The Bitter Cry of Outcast London*, London 1883

Morrison, Arthur: *A Child of the Jago*, London 1896

Norman, Philip: *London Vanished and Vanishing*, A&C Black, 1905

Miele, Chris (ed): *From William Morris: Building Conservation and the Arts & Crafts Cult of Authenticity 1877-1939*, Yale University Press 2005

Pevsner, N: *The Buildings of England: London Volumes 1-6*, Yale

Preston, William C: *The Bitter Cry of Outcast London*, James Clarke & Co Ltd, 1883

Pulley, Judy: *Streets of the City*, Capital History 2006

Rasmussen, Steen Eiler: *London: The Unique City*, The MIT Press 1934

Royston Pike, E: *Human Documents of the Industrial Revolution in Britain*, Routledge 1966

Service, Alastair: *London 1900*, Granada 1979

Shelley, Henry: *Inns & Taverns of Old London*, Pitman 1909

Sheppard, Francis: *London 1808-1870: The Infernal Wen*, Secker & Warburg 1971

Stamp, Gavin: *Britain's Lost Cities*, Aurum 2007

Stamp, Gavin: *The Changing Metropolis: Earliest Photographs of London 1839-1879*, Viking 1984

Stamp, Gavin: *Lost Victorian Britain*, Aurum 2010

Stuart Gray, A: *Edwardian Architecture*, Wordsworth 1985

Summerson, John: *Georgian London*, Barrie & Jenkins 1988

Szreter, Simon and Mooney, Graham: *Urbanisation, mortality and the standard of living debate*, Economic History Review, Vol. 51 February 1998

Survey of London: Various volumes

Thurston-Hopkins, R: *This London, Its Taverns, Haunts & Memories*, Cecil Palmer 1927

Walford, Edward: *Old and New London*, Cassell & Co 1897

Waller, Maureen: *Life in the Debris of War*, St Martin's Press 2005

Weightman, Gavin & Humphries, Steve: *The Making of Modern London 1815-1914*, Sidgwick & Jackson 1983

Weinreb, Ben & Hibbert, Christopher: *The London Encyclopaedia*, Macmillan 1983

Wheatley, Henry & Cunningham, Peter: *London Past & Present* (3 vols), John Murray 1891

White, Jerry: *London in the 20th Century*, Vintage Books: 2008

Whitehouse, Roger: *A London Album*, Secker & Warburg 1980

Williams, A E: *Barnardo of Stepney*, Allen & Unwin 1943

Winder, Robert: *Bloody Foreigners*, Little, Brown 2004

Yee, Chiang: *The Silent Traveller in London*, 1938

Left: 7-12 Stockwell Street, 1911

The heart of Greenwich and the source of its water supply. The town well was close by and several old wells have been found in the vicinity. A good group of 17th century weatherboarded houses with bracketed timber cornices and steeply-pitched clay tile roofs.

47 Paternoster Row, 17 August 1908
A fine late 17th century house that was typical of many in the area. The angled boards on the fronts of many of the houses are mirrors to reflect light into the windows above – once a common feature of the narrow alleyways of the City.